HV   Barnard, Charles P $16.50
5276
.B37   Families, alcoholism, and
            therapy.

FAMILIES, ALCOHOLISM AND THERAPY

By

CHARLES P. BARNARD, Ed.D.

Graduate Program Director
Marriage and Family Therapy
University of Wisconsin at Stout
Menomonie, Wisconsin

CHARLES C THOMAS • PUBLISHER
Springfield • Illinois • U.S.A.

Published and Distributed Throughout the World by
CHARLES C THOMAS • PUBLISHER
Bannerstone House
301-327 East Lawrence Avenue, Springfield, Illinois, U.S.A.

© *1981, by* CHARLES C THOMAS • PUBLISHER
ISBN 0-398-04173-3(pbk.)
Library of Congress Catalog Card Number: 80 22568

*With THOMAS BOOKS careful attention is given to all details of
manufacturing and design. It is the Publisher's desire to present books that are
satisfactory as to their physical qualities and artistic possibilities and appropriate for their particular use. THOMAS BOOKS will be true to those laws of
quality that assure a good name and good will.*

Barnard, Charles P
   Families, alcoholism, and therapy.

   Bibliography: p.
   Includes index.
   1. Alcoholics—Rehabilitation.   2. Alcoholism—Treatment.   3. Family psycho-
therapy.   4. Alcoholics—Family relationships.   I.   Title.
[DNLM: 1. Alcoholism—Therapy.   2. Family therapy.   WM274 B259f]
HV5276.B37   362.8′2   80-22568
ISBN 0-398-04157-1
ISBN 0-398-04173-3 (pbk.)

Printed in the United States of America
PS-R-1

PREFACE

THIS book was written with the hope that more people might become involved in assisting the alcoholic and family in their difficult recovery process. I have been allowed to observe large numbers of these families journey through recovery, and I believe my life has been enriched by the experience and hope that the impact was reciprocal. The client population about which this book is written was a "forgotten and forsaken group" for many years. I am pleased to know that at this point they are receiving necessary and deserving attention.

While the writing of this book has been a worthwhile personal experience, it was not done in isolation and many "thank yous" are in order. Joanne Fruit and Bel Brockman are to be thanked for their typing, especially in light of my schedule, which always seemed to be best exemplified by, "I need it by yesterday." I also wish to thank Dr. Carlyle Gilbertson, chairperson of the Department of Counseling and Psychological Services at the University of Wisconsin-Stout, for his understanding and support in this venture. Mr. Rob Ernst is deserving of acknowledgment for his idea regarding the title of this book. As I struggled with many alternatives it was Rob who offered one of his "simple solutions."

I want to finish these prefatory comments by stating my hope that this book will facilitate "helpers" in being of greater assistance to the estimated group of 40 million alcoholics and family members.

C.P.B.

INTRODUCTION

FOR some years now, alcoholism has been referred to as a "family illness." In spite of this, I have encountered too many cases wherein the family was only given transitory consideration which I believe is not only counterproductive for them but for the identified alcoholic and the difficult recovery process as well. While AA, Alanon, and Alateen have done bountiful work, my concern is that the family as a connected and operational whole has gone unnoticed for the most part. It is my contention that many families have been unnecessarily sacrificed in order to achieve and maintain sobriety. As this is the case, I also believe many individuals have unnecessarily sacrificed their sobriety in order to maintain their tenuous and brittle family relationships. This book is designed to help individuals perceive alcoholism as a family illness from a general systems orientation in a way which can avoid these unnecessary sacrifices in the recovery process. The ability of family therapy to accomplish this resulted in Keller (*Second Special Report to the U.S. Congress on Alcohol and Health*, 1974) stating the following about involving families in the alcoholism treatment process: "It (family therapy) is the most notable current advance in the area of psychotherapy (of alcoholism)."

While the book is directed to those involved in the alcohol and other drug abuse (AODA) treatment field, I believe other professionals, less well informed about AODA issues could also benefit. It is now well documented that in mental health consultation rooms across the United States, alcoholism is confounding human problems being discussed but continues to go unnoticed as a problem in and of itself. Along with recognition of alcoholism as a problem, this book is intended to highlight the intimate connection of the alcoholic with the family and what treatment from this perspective entails.

In Chapter 1, the reader will find an overview of the magnitude of alcoholism as a problem and it's pervasive effects upon all involved. The reader is also presented with some significant research regarding the role of family therapy in the treatment of alcoholism. This chapter was designed to establish the connection and natural treatment link of alcoholism and families.

Chapter 2 identifies frequently observed characteristics of families where alcoholism exists. Case examples are frequently utilized to illustrate the theoretical constructs discussed. Certainly the reader familiar with the alcoholic population will think of many other illustrations as this chapter is digested.

As Chapter 2 discussed major theoretical constructs, Chapter 3 is designed to translate the theory of Chapter 2 into treatment action. Along with the identification of specific interventions for alcoholics and their families, a broader perspective of strategies for change is also presented.

Chapter 4 focuses upon the reciprocal adjustment of family and alcoholic to the downward spiral of the progressive nature of alcoholism. Along with the progressive stages of this process, attention is also devoted to the difficult task of engaging all family members into the treatment process.

Adolescent alcohol and other drug abuse is the focus of Chapter 5. It seems appropriate for adolescents to receive special consideration in light of the estimation of there being 3.3 million problem drinkers in the 14-17 year age range (*NIAAA/IFS*, Nov. 30, 1978, p. 1). In consideration of the adolescent's attempts to separate from the family while yet maintaining the connection, family therapy of the adolescent problem drinker appears even more obvious. Implications for treating the adolescent and family are presented in Chapter 5.

Chapter 6 presents an evaluation process developed by the author. The process has demonstrated itself to be a valuable process for not only diagnostic purposes, but as a means of engaging families in the treatment process as well. The author hopes the readers can take this process and, in combination with their own creativeness, find it a valuable tool in providing more efficient services to alcoholics and their families.

Sex receives separate attention in Chapter 7. A chapter devoted to the relationship of sex and alcohol seemed appropriate in light of the author's experience of sex being a prominent problem in nearly 100 percent of the marriages where one or the other, if not both, of the spouses was alcoholic.

The last chapter—Chapter 8—is devoted to the utilization of the group process in the treatment of alcoholic marriages and families. The group process seems to be almost universally utilized in the treatment of alcoholism, and certainly much of the success of AA can be attributed to the wise fashion in which group phenomena have been employed. Special attention is devoted to what appears to be appropriate goals for groups of couples brought together in the interest of facilitating the recovery process. More specific concerns of implementation of group treatment are also addressed in this chapter.

While this book is certainly not all inclusive, it does reflect this author's perceptions of important variables to consider in the treatment of alcoholism. As mentioned earlier, the author hopes as these perceptions are shared that the reader is enriched and becomes better prepared to help this group that for so long was "forgotten and forsaken."

CONTENTS

FAMILIES, ALCOHOLISM AND THERAPY

Chapter 1

ALCOHOLISM AND THE FAMILY

INTRODUCTION

O N a post-treatment basis, all too often we observe the recovering alcoholic either resuming old drinking patterns and/or his family dissolving as he maintains sobriety. While there are many hypotheses offered as explanation for this occurrence, the one that appears to be surfacing as most prominent is the acknowledgment of alcoholism as a "family illness." The inference of the term *family illness* is that everyone is involved in mutually maintaining and simultaneously being affected by it. The analogy of a mobile may be best used to illustrate the construct being identified here. As a mobile hangs motionless from a ceiling, the touching of any one element results in all others being stimulated and manifesting the results of one being activated. It is as though none of the mobile's elements can go unaffected when any of the others are upset. It is this very phenomena that occurs in the families with which this book is concerned.

Today's literature seems to suggest that this country's population of alcoholics numbers from 9.3 to 10 million in the adult population (*NIAAA/IFS*, November 30, 1978, p. 1). Assuming this to be true, and going on to conservatively assume that each alcoholic is involved with, on the average, two others (spouse and one child), we can quickly determine that we are talking about a population of 28-30 million. And this figure does not account for the estimated 3.3 million problem drinkers in the 14-17 age range (*NIAAA/IFS*, November 30, 1978, p. 1). By anyone's standards this is a significant proportion of our population. Certainly anyone that has had contact with alcoholism is also aware that this portion of the population is probably as shattered and debilitated by contact with it as all those who have preceded them. The human suffering of these people and their treatment is also what this book hopes to address itself to.

While there have been many different treatment approaches attempted with alcoholism, the family modality is one of the newer ones and also one that seems to offer significant promise. In fact, in the *Second Special Report to the U.S. Congress on Alcohol and Health*, (Keller, 1974), family therapy as a treatment modality for alcoholism was referred to as "the most notable current advance in the area of psychotherapy (of alcoholism)." The validity of the family, as a focus of treatment, seems to have been adequately documented in Steinglass' (Steinglass, 1976) article, which surveys research covering the period from 1950 to 1975. While this is an exhaustive review, there are also numerous other independent studies in the literature that identify the efficacy and effectiveness of family treatment. All one needs to do is review the National Institute on Alcohol Abuse and Alcoholism's (NIAAA) Information and Feature Service issues; it is quickly realized that there is barely an issue published without reference to a family orientation to alcoholism treatment. This is especially true over the last three years.

The focus of this book is thus on treatment that involves the entire family, and the focus is kept on them as a unit throughout all the dimensions of treatment and recovery. All too often the author has spoken with those providers of treatment to alcoholics who define a family focus as involving the nonalcoholic spouse in the treatment regimen for perhaps three days. This involvement of the nonalcoholic spouse may then be buttressed by one or two individual sessions with the same nonalcoholic spouse. The only way the children are even tangentially involved is as a source of inducing guilt in the alcoholic. It is this type of "family focused treatment" that the author believes is a prostitution of the concept of treating the entire family.

Even more appalling than the constricted view just identified is the view espoused by some that the alcoholic should sever ties with the family. The other alcoholics being treated, along with the helpers, then become a surrogate family. Assuming that the alcoholic is then likely to manifest behaviors similar to what were operationalized in the family, and these behaviors can be confronted and changed—is this success? What happens to the alcoholic upon return to the family, assuming it is still there after treatment? Without attention and efforts to help the whole family change, it seems only reasonable to expect difficulties. It is as though the alcoholic's language (behavior) has been changed and the family is expected to speak the same language even though they have not had similar educational opportunities. It is not unrealistic to expect that potential for contact between the alcoholic and family are minimal at best. It is this approach that epitomizes the idea of the "sick individual," which Dr. Albert Pawlowski, chief of the NIAAA Extramural Research Branch, is addressing in the following statement: "The attention being given the family treatment represents a promising new thrust in a field where the emphasis has traditionally been the "sick alcoholic persons"' (*NIAAA/IFS*, April 12, 1976, p. 2).

Perhaps Kaufman and Kaufman have most succinctly captured the role of the family in the treatment of drug abusers and addicts. The following are observations they identify as "recurring phenomena which demonstrate that the family is part of the solution as well as the problem and, therefore, must be part of the treatment from the beginning."

1. Addicts tend to replicate old familial patterns in their new environment through the roles they assume in the TC (therapeutic community) family as in past close dyadic and triadic relationships.
2. Internalized feelings about family members, such as rage, helplessness at being controlled, or yearning for nurturance, inhibit the patient's growth. These feelings can more easily be uncovered or worked through with the real family.
3. Families frequently sabotage treatment through a variety of consciously or unconsciously determined mechanisms which, if untreated, result in the family encouraging elopements and the use of drugs and alcohol.
4. Family systems exert tremendous pull or suction upon the lives of their members. If the old system, which helped produce the addict, is not changed, the addict will respond to the existing system suction by returning to drug use

upon completing or splitting from the TC. (Kaufman and Kaufmann, 1977, pp. 468-469).

In talking with various helpers, who operate from one or the other of the above identified postures, it has become apparent to me that the primary reason for not including the entire family is lack of information/understanding. This book was written in an effort to try and increase the level of information for those in the position of helping.

It seems that implementation of family therapy principles in alcoholism treatment not only increases treatment effectiveness with the alcoholic but can also help the family recalibrate itself in such a way that sobriety can be more assured and all members of the family can more productively move beyond the uncomfortable places they have been. Perhaps the findings of a study by Coleman and Davis, financed by the National Institute on Drug Abuse, best captures the impact of family therapy on dependent individuals and their families. In this study, they surveyed 500 clinics providing services in the drug abuse field. Part of their survey involved interviewing some of the families receiving family therapy. Coleman and Davis state the following about those interviewed: "Those who were seen were highly positive about the personal effects of family therapy and viewed it as a major determinant in changing their addictive patterns. Some expressed the wish that it (family therapy) had been introduced much earlier in their treatment" (Coleman and Davis, 1978, p. 28).

The author also believes the operationalization of a family therapy focus can provide essential preventive aspects. There are significant studies that point out the greater likelihood of children of alcoholics becoming alcoholics themselves (Goodwin, 1971; Goodwin, Schulsinger, Hermansen, Guze, and Winokur, 1973). It is through family therapy, with involvement of the children, that the youngsters can better understand what has happened and learn about how people and families can function in a dependent, free state. It is this dimension of prevention that provides new excitement for the individual working from the family orientation. The results of sessions with this family will be manifested not in just the immediate years but also in the generations to follow. It seems that for this reason Dr. William

Bosma, Director of the Division of Alcoholism and Drug Abuse, University of Maryland Hospital, pointed to the need for a vast increase in the availability of family therapists in alcoholism treatment (*NIAAA/IFS,* July 14, 1974, p. 4).

Even though the application of family therapy to alcoholism treatment is relatively recent in origin, there has been reference to the family and the connection to alcoholism for many years. Both Knight (1937) and Chassell (1938) emphasized the importance of understanding the total family situation in order to more fully comprehend the individual's drinking behavior. In more recent years clinicians have reported that in some families, the well-being of other family members seemed to be dependent upon the alcoholic's continual drinking, in others the nonalcoholic spouse began to decompensate as the drinking member got better; and that drinking relapses were influenced by the re-entry of a recovering alcoholic into a family that had not changed in accordance with the change of the alcoholic (Bailey, 1968).

EFFECTS IN THE FAMILY

The preventive aspect just referred to takes on special significance when the ramifications of the alcoholic family system are examined more closely. At this point, attention will go beyond the dollar figure that alcohol abuse and alcoholism cost the nation ($43 billion in 1975; the most recent year for which estimates are available) and focus on the human manifestations for which dollars cannot be attached.

Physical-Emotional on Children

In a recent study it was determined that physical violence is more than twice as likely to occur in families with alcohol problems as opposed to those without (Byles, 1978). Naturally, the targets of this familial violence are the nonalcoholic spouse and/or children. Depending upon the anger and rage precipitated, the severity of the damage is determined. This lack of adaptive, constructive means of expressing aggression is an often observed phenomena in the alcoholic families. The lack of mechanisms for constructive expression seems to make these rages more understandable when we consider the reduction of inhibitions promulgated by the affects of the alcohol. Experience in a special program for children of alcoholics in Silver Spring, Maryland has demonstrated that feelings of anger are among those most commonly expressed by these youngsters in the safety of this environment (*NIAAA/IFS*, March 3, 1978, p. 6). It is as though this is one of the few places they have in their world where it is appropriate to express anger. Naturally, without the opportunity to express it, and then learning how to cope with this feeling constructively, it is unfair to assume this adaptive behavior would just occur on its own. A safe assumption seems to be that these children of alcoholic families have probably not had adequate adult models demonstrating adaptive expression of aggression in their family setting.

Other research also documents difficulty with aggression being manifested by children from alcoholic families. The researchers from the West Philadelphia Clinic have said: "Compared with normal children, those in a family with parental alcoholism are less able to maintain attention, less responsive to environmental stimulation, and much more prone to emotional upset. They tend to be anxious, fearful individuals who have great difficulty in containing or regulating their excitement or mood. They are subject to aggressive behavior and show evidence of deficient learning of certain moral codes of conduct" (*NIAAA/IFS*, October 10, 1975, p. 4). This study went on to document that while children of parents with psychological difficulties manifested similar behavior, it was not to the same degree as those children from alcoholic families.

Similar findings have been reported in Baltimore, Maryland where 60 percent of all children seen at a pediatric behavioral clinic had an alcoholic parent (*NIAAA/IFS*, July 14, 1974, p. 4). These behaviors seem to be a manifestation of the state of these children, referred to as "emotional orphans," in another report (*NIAAA/IFS*, April 1, 1975, p. 3). This report goes on to identify how often it is observed that children in alcoholic families are induced into being a pseudo-wife/husband or pseudo-mother/father to replace the alcoholic parent(s). Nagy and Spark (1973) identify this process as *parentification* and elaborate extensively about the pervasive negative effects of this occurrence upon the children. Even if the children are not parentified, because of the ineptness of the alcoholic spouse and the frequent obsession of the nonalcoholic spouse with the alcoholic behavior, there is just not time nor energy for the children and they become "emotional orphans."

Incest is another way in which children in a family with an alcoholic parent are jeopardized. In a recent study it was concluded that as many as 75 percent of adult incest perpetrators are alcoholics (Meiselmen, 1978). There is a bountiful amount of literature that documents the injurious effects of incest upon the child participant in the forms of negative self-esteem, inordinate guilt, retarded sexual development with prominent residual impact once the child is an adult, more negative sibling relationships and so on. The prominence of incest among families with an alcoholic parent should come as no surprise when considering elements characteristic of this family, such as: the parental sexual relationship deteriorates and sexual dysfunctions predominate; sex comes to be regarded as a convenient means of expressing covert hostility; sexual put-downs, lack of compassion, and an unwillingness to give to one another increases; denial becomes rampant in the family system and generalizes to moral codes and social mores once valued (just as the denial plays a key role in the stimulation of the incestuous behavior, it also serves to keep the behavior from becoming confronted and resolved); the alcohol results in reduction of normal inhibitory anxieties; and generational boundaries between the adults and kids become blurred and a child is utilized to fulfill needs normally satisfied in the adult subsystem. It is surprising when considering the similarities between families with an alcoholic parent and those families where incest is manifested in the absence of alcohol or other chemical usage.

An older study, but nonetheless in significance, demonstrated that children of alcoholic families report the following: they suffered both in familial relationships and in relationships external to the family; their school work was seriously affected; nearly all reported feeling unwanted by either one or both parents, and two-thirds of these children felt angry and hostile toward their parents and other adults; and most also indicated feeling ashamed, anxious, easily upset and deficient in self-confidence (Cork, 1969).

Experience also demonstrates the way in which unusual tensions and animosities are developed among siblings in alcoholic families. If relationships do develop, they often border on the pathological out of their intense need for one another. It becomes quite apparent that while the family should be the workshop for developing interpersonal skills, very few are developed in the alcoholic families beyond those that do more than promote basic survival.

Along with the physical damage incurred during rageful outbursts, another physical ramification of alcoholism or abusive drinking patterns is the *fetal alcohol syndrome*. Dr. Eileen Quelletle, conducting research at the Boston City Hospital, has determined significant ramifications of drinking among pregnant women (*NIAAA/IFS*, July 29, 1976, p. 4). She identified three separate groups among 559 women studied. Fifty percent of the population were abstinent or rare drinkers (Group 1), 40 percent drank moderately (Group 2), and 10 percent were heavy drinkers (Group 3). It was determined that 63 percent of the babies of Group 3 mothers showed neurological abnormalities, in contrast to 23 percent of the babies of Group 1 and 26 percent of the Group 2 mothers. Recent figures identify the fetal alcohol syndrome as the third leading cause of birth defects with associated mental retardation, following only Down's syndrome and spina bifida (*NIAAA/IFS*, November 30, 1978, p. 4). Of these three conditions, the Fetal Alcohol Syndrome is the only one that is preventable.

While one could go on identifying further reports, with similarly distressing findings, it seems the above reports adequately document the potential effect upon children of the alcoholic family. While there are children, that have one or both parents with alcohol problems, who seem to leave the family unscathed, there is a significant proportion who suffer the consequences and may pay the price for the rest of their lives.

Marriage

There are a number of studies that document the frequency with which divorce and alcoholism, or alcohol problems, are reported concurrently. Kephart (1954) reported that of the 1,434 divorces randomly selected from a Philadelphia court, 21 percent reported drinking as the primary reason for divorce. Straus and Bacon (1951) reported that 27 percent of the 2,023 male alcoholics being treated in outpatient clinics were divorced as opposed to 7 percent of the general population at the time of the study. More recently, Towle (1974) reported that 53 percent of a population of 2,239 pateints from a public inebriate program were divorced (97% male) as opposed to a 4.6 percent figure of males divorced in the general population at the time of the 1970 census. While one could continue on with the report of studies with similar findings, it seems sufficient to utilize the above as testimony to the "strange bedfellows," which alcoholism and marriage seem to make.

While it is common knowledge regarding the potential havoc that can be created by divorce upon all involved, recent figures also identify that among women under age thirty-five, the highest incidence of problem drinking occurs among those who are divorced or separated (*NIAAA/IFS*, November 30, 1978, p. 1). Edwards et al. (1973) have identified what they referred to as "disturbed personality theories." This being the evidence of the wife, as nonalcoholic spouse, manifesting psychosocial problems, mental decompensation, or her attempts to sabotage improvement when her husband shows signs of controlling his drinking. Certainly none of these behaviors are such that they would be defined as positive in nature.

FAMILY THERAPY AND ALCOHOLISM

The early emphasis on treating the family as opposed to just the identified patient, or the individual manifesting disturbance, came out of the study of schizophrenia. It was from these early studies by individuals such as Don Jackson, Gregory Bateson, and others that an intense awareness of the family's involvement in human difficulties and their maintenance became prominent. The realization that the family functions as other systems do has had a profound impact on the conceptualization and treatment of psychological difficulties. These same insights are now being applied to the area of alcoholism treatment, and it is becoming more common to observe facilities adding this treatment dimension. Dr. David Berenson has identified the "adaptive consequences" of drinking for family stability and functioning and how these adaptive consequences are sufficiently reinforcing to maintain problem drinking in light of the apparent negative consequences (Berenson, 1976). The family as the focus seems to be responsive to the statement: "The dry is as sick as the drunk, except that the bodily damage is not there" (Johnson, V.E., 1973, p. 30). It is with this acknowledgment of the whole family being involved, and with a concern for them, that they are encouraged into treatment.

While family therapy, as a recent dimension of alcoholism treatment, should not be regarded as a panacea, there are numerous reports of its success in the literature. A program at the University of Maryland Hospital is utilizing family treatment and the Director, Dr. Marvin Kamback, comments: "If the family develops more functional ways of interacting, it will be easier for individual members to solve their particular problems, including alcoholism. We have had cases where the alcoholism simply disappears without specific treatment of the alcoholic member when the family begins to function better" (*NIAAA/IFS*, January 7, 1976, p. 5).

The Palm Beach Institute—an alcoholism treatment unit which gained public notoriety by treating the ex-Congressman Wilbur Mills—has even coined the term *familization therapy* to describe their orientation (*NIAAA/IFS*, September 19, 1975, p. 3). The Institute's treatment approach involves admitting the patient's family as co-patients to the facility. This approach is based upon the theory that the "malfunctioning of the patient's family is a major contributing factor in the emotional or behavioral dysfunctioning that leads to problem habits like drinking."

Another program that relies upon family therapy as its primary treatment orientation has reported interesting findings. The Family Alcoholism Care and Treatment (FACT) program of Dayton, Ohio attempts to deal initially with the family crisis invoked by the alcoholic's behavior before the total collapse of the family occurs. The experience of this program suggests that the family approach identifies the alcoholic and draws them into treatment at an earlier stage than traditional programs aimed at seeing the individual alcoholic do. In a comparison of the alcoholic persons identified in the FACT program with those enrolled in the local county's acute care alcoholism program, FACT clients were found to be, on the average, about ten years younger. The officials of the project reported the following in their evaluation report regarding this ten years difference: "This is of extreme importance because in many cases that ten-year difference is the difference between repairable pathological damage and irreparable pathological damage" (*NIAAA/IFS*, April 26, 1975, p. 1).

SUMMARY

These various reports on implementation of family therapy in treating alcoholism have as a common thread the construct of the family as a system. This infers that changing a family member in isolation from the family may be ineffectual and/or destructive to the family. To consolidate gains made by the alcoholic, and in order to minimize the risk of relapse, the total family system must be assisted to change. As this is a relatively recent approach as far as actual implementation, there must be concern for not "throwing the baby out with the wash water." By this statement, acknowledgment is meant to be given to Alcoholics Anonymous (AA) and the success it has identified with its name in the field of alcoholism treatment. As mentioned earlier, it would be ridiculous to identify with family therapy as a panacea to alcoholism treatment and thereby brush aside an approach with the validity that years of experience with the AA approach has demonstrated it to have. Rather, what this author strongly advocates is a combination of the AA and family therapy approaches. It is this author's contention that the two together have a definite synergistic effect with one another. It seems that these two together can surpass what either might accomplish individually. The end result of this synergism can then begin to have an impact upon the ugliness of this albatross to society and the millions of individuals it affects.

Chapter 2

ALCOHOLIC FAMILIES AS A SYSTEM

INTRODUCTION

In a *Family System Approach to Alcoholism*, Bowen (1974) observes that the focus is on *what* happened, *how* it happened, and *when* and *where* it happened, insofar as observations are made on fact. It carefully avoids man's automatic preoccupation with *why* it happened. In that context, the therapist is concerned with reciprocal actions, reactions, ways of relating, communicating, and meeting needs in a given family (Meeks, 1976, p. 843).

THIS quote identifies the concerns of the therapist intervening from a "systems point of view." The intention of this chapter is to identify and describe the kinds of elements characteristic of families that the family therapist is alert to for purposes of assessment, intervention, and the resultant evaluation. The elements to be discussed are found in all family systems, but examples from alcoholic families will be used for purposes of illustration.

"SYSTEMNESS"

At its most basic, the concept of a system denotes a number of parts that are relatively organized so that a change in one or more parts is usually accompanied by a change in the other parts of a system (Bertalanffy, 1966). The family, as a system, connotes the idea that the members are mutually interdependent and interacting. As one changes, the effects of that change ripple out and affect the others, just as a pebble dropped in one place of a pool of water creates ripples, which affect the entire area.

14

Imagine the family wherein the father frequently abuses alcohol. He enters the house inebriated, and the wife reacts with angry shrills. The husband meets her confrontation with equal anger and velocity. This wakes the youngest child who begins to scream. This wakes the next oldest who runs out to intervene with the combative parents. The oldest child continues to sleep and internalizes the external confusion into a nightmare. The crying baby, and intervening middle child, amplify the parents difficulty as the mother accuses the father of having precipitated all this, and the father retaliates with similar accusations regarding her loud outburst directed at him upon entering the house. The father hits the mother and retires to the couch while she returns to the bedroom with her two youngest children to nurture and be nurtured. The oldest child sleeps on.

The next morning the father leaves the house without sharing a word, while the mother proceeds to be oversolicitous of her children who she believes should not be exposed to such chaos. The oldest child goes to school and sits, unable to concentrate on the work at hand, due to an all consuming preoccupation with the nightmare of last night.

During the day the frustration builds for both parents as they seem unable to get out of the pattern. The husband's frustration leads him to feel a need for "a quick one" after work, and the mother's frustration results in her being unable to control her anger when he returns inebriated again that night. The children's concern for their parents' future intensifies, and they become more clinging, or act out the confusion, frustration, and anger they experience. Here the two most significant adult persons in their life are unable to solve their problems, thereby leaving the children with the generalized belief that this world must indeed be a tenuous place at best. The younger children begin to manifest disturbed behavior, and the oldest child begins to fail his courses and manifest behavioral disturbance in the classroom. The children's behavior intensifies the bitterness and distance between the parents, which amplifies both the mother's angry diatribes and the father's drinking. The vicious cycle begins to act like a runaway equation and seems out of control at this time as this family spins along on its destructive path.

In presenting this example, the first element presented was that of the drunken father entering the house. Hopefully the reader realizes that the example could have been initiated just as easily with an attacking mother, and/or disturbing or disturbed children as the precipitating variable. The following example may serve to graphically portray this construct.

The Vicious Cycle

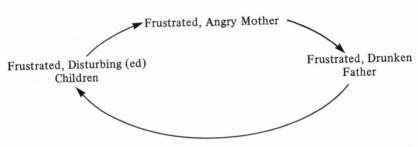

The cycle could be stimulated into action by the behavior of any one of the components. They are indeed interconnected via their mutual, reciprocal interaction and interdependence. To attempt to determine who is at fault can be an impossible task at best. What is evident is that this process is occurring in this family and to the detriment of all involved. Naturally, by saying to the detriment of all involved, there is the inferred assumption that people do not care to be frustrated, bitter, angry, and feeling distanced from one another. To this writer, this seems to be a safe assumption.

From the preceding, the reader may now have a better sense of the analogy of the family to a suspended mobile. As the mobile hangs motionless, the activation of any one element results in all the others being simultaneously affected. This is as it is in the alcoholic family of consideration in this book.

ROLES

Another characteristic of families as systems is that of roles. All families have roles to be filled, such as breadwinner, parent, spouse, homemaker, and others. Families also have emotional roles that are filled/assigned. Paolino and McCrady have stated the following regarding emotional roles:

> Families may also have roles such as "troublemaker," "denier," or "calm decision maker." Many families also include the role of the

sick patient, which is often the role of the alcoholic in an alcoholic marriage. That is, the family structure would require that one member of the family not function capably, according to his supposed abilities, and rather would engage in unpredictable, socially unacceptable behaviors. This role might allow others in the family to assume the role of caretaker, knowing parent, or angry accuser. Systems theory emphasizes that any system requires a variety of roles in order to function (Paolino and McCrady, 1977, pp. 111-112).

We can describe a role as a more or less related set of expectations attached to a position in the family. These expectations may be discovered to be of either a conscious or unconscious nature. To illustrate this let us refer to the above quotation from Paolino and McCrady. The husband/father in this example drinks initially because it is his "conscious" choice; or is it because this is his expectation of the breadwinner's role as a result of his experience with his own father and more generally with males in general in the culture from which he has come; or could it be that an expectation of his wife's self-perceived role is that of caretaker of her husband, and in order to fulfill this self-perceived role, she needs a man that drinks such as her father did?

This example also serves to underline the reciprocal nature of roles in families and punctuates the systemness of the family. The following quote elaborates on this idea:

For every role, there is a reciprocal role in at least one other position. The husband's role as sex partner, for example, is inconceivable without the spouse's reciprocal role as his sex partner, and vice versa. The companionship role is again unintelligible apart from a companionship role in another family member, spouse or child. The disciplinarian role presupposes the existence of one who is the object of the discipline. When one of those roles is not performed as expected by one or more of the family members, at least one other family member is affected. When it is realized that a family is generally composed of several members, each of whom performs a good many roles that are intricately interwoven in a network of reciprocally related roles, the systemness of the family can begin to be grasped (Barnard and Corrales, 1979, p. 8).

RULES

Rules are the glue or skeleton of the family structure. The rules are the primary determinant or governor of the roles family members occupy, although there is a reciprocal interaction between these two. Certainly we are all aware of rules such as who takes out the garbage and how often, who does the dishes, mows the lawn, and other similar rules regarding tasks and behaviors. To the family therapist, rules of a more subtle nature are of particular concern in assessment for formulating interventions. Dodson and Kurpius (1977) have identified a number of areas, important to family dysfunctioning, about which families determine rules of the nature being considered here.

When and how may a member go away from this family to relate to others? It may be that the husband who goes out singly with friends drinks to submerge the realization that he broke a family rule of leaving without the others. Perhaps the wife drinks when the husband leaves to numb her hurt regarding the sense of rejection stemming from the husband breaking the rule.

Another example of an area about which families have rules is that of how one may show feelings such as love, hurt, or anger and how one may receive those feelings from another. This is a very prominent concern for those working with alcoholic families. All too often those who work with these families are aware of the difficulty that love and anger pose: The husband who feels that he can only express anger when he is intoxicated or the husband and wife who seem to be in an unconscious agreement that intoxication is the only way anger can be expressed by one or both, or the same type of agreement/rule which, while never spoken by the couple, is ever present and only allows for affection being expressed while one or both are under the influence.

Other areas where rules are formulated for family functioning are: What, when, and how may one comment on what one sees, feels, and thinks; who can speak to whom and about what may we speak; how can one be different; how may one express sexuality; how can one be male or female and when; how can a person acquire self worth and how much is it appropriate to possess. If, for example, the rule is that the husband cannot possess more self-esteem than the wife, abusive drinking on his part may seem to restore equilibrium to their relationship when he begins to enhance his own sense of worth and competence. The drinking results in him feeling less worthwhile, and the relationship rule, although never spoken, has been honored. Rules are central to providing a sense of equilibrium or homeostasis to the family system.

HOMEOSTASIS

Equilibrium, or homeostasis, is understood as being important to any type of system, families included. This construct is particularly important to those working with the alcoholic family. It is the homeostatic force that seems to account for the example cited at the outset of this book, wherein the alcoholic completes what appears to be a very successful treatment and returns to his family only to resume the old drinking patterns. The family had developed a sense of equilibrium with his drinking as a central role. With his returning as a more stable, assertive, and functional member, the family's homeostasis has been upset. Mother is required to not be as over-responsible, the adolescent son is no longer able to have his close and favored relationship with his mother, resulting in his abusing the younger children who have been left alone, and so on. The family had calibrated itself in such a way that equilibrium was maintained with the father as a drunkard.

Without help we can be most assured that the father will return to old drinking patterns or perhaps the family will dissolve as a result of his resolve not to assume his old role and abide by the old rules of him as a drinker. Another possibility is that some other member will decompensate and fill the role he assumed as an active alcoholic, thereby allowing the family to move on with the same roles, only reassigned. Naturally the family may go ahead and muster enough resources to break out of their old homeostatic set and recalibrate themselves in such a way that alcohol abuse is no longer necessary to maintain itself. The writer believes that without professional help in this recalibration process, the family is in, at best, for a long and arduous task in their journey to establish a new homeostasis. Naturally, more functional families have the capacity to recalibrate themselves via changing rules, roles, and other dimensions in order to accommodate to stress and change. These more functional families have effective negotiation skills and other resources which facilitate their adapting without symptomatic behavior being manifested in the system.

BOUNDARIES

The characteristic of boundaries in families is another construct important to understand as we move from homeostasis. Just as the roles and rules are vital to the maintenance of homeostasis, so are the boundaries that characterize the relationships. The one individual who has written most extensively about boundaries is Salvador Minuchin:

> The function of boundaries is to protect the differentiation of the system. Every family subsystem has specific functions and makes specific demands on its members; and the development of interpersonal skills achieved in these subsystems is predicated on the subsystems freedom from interference by other subsystems. For example, the capacity for complementary accommodation between spouses requires freedom from interference by in-laws and children and sometimes by the extra familial. The development of skills for negotiating with peers, learned among siblings, requires noninterference from parents (Minuchin, 1974, pp. 53-54).

Minuchin has identified three primary types of boundaries: enmeshed, clear, and disengaged. He believes, as does this writer, that boundaries reside between every subsystem in the family. Keep in mind that examples of subsystems in the family are the parental subsystem, sibling subsystem, father and sons subsystems, mother-daughter subsystem, father-oldest child subsystem, and so on. Also, each individual in the family comprises a separate subsystem.

Family Boundaries

enmeshed   clear   disengaged
. . . . - - - - - - - - - - - - - - - - -─────────────

Clear boundaries are those that result in the most functional relationships. Relationships with clear boundaries provide room for separateness, but yet have the capacity for closeness as well. Communications are open and direct. Individuals in these relationships are given freedom and return it to those they are involved with just as they do respect and concern.

Enmeshed boundaries characterize those relationships where

differentness or separateness are not allowed. To be different is regarded as being disloyal. Individual boundaries are blurred, and the relationship absorbs the individuals that constitute it into an amorphous, blob-like conglomeration. It has been the experience of this writer that many times adolescent abusers are from a family characterized by this type of boundary development. The adolescent feels suffocated and lost and seems to turn to chemicals to numb the senses and/or break a supreme family rule, almost as if expulsion is desired. The adolescent is aware of no other way to "escape the clutches" of this family and develop greater autonomy and individuality. Individuals in the family with enmeshed boundaries have a strong sense of belongingness, but little, if any, sense of separateness.

The last type of boundary to be discussed, and another often observed in alcoholic families, is the disengaged type. This type of boundary is overly rigid, and communication between subsystems with this boundary type is difficult, if at all possible. In families with this boundary type, separateness is developed, but the individuals possess little, if any, sense of belongingness. This type of boundary is often observed in families of adolescent abusers who use chemicals to numb their sense of aloneness and/or in an effort to get other family members to notice and attend to them. Spouses often will manifest disengaged boundaries as they have pulled away from one another and have very little, if any, contact physically, emotionally, and/or via verbal communication. Just as this lack of contact may have resulted from the abusive drinking, it may also serve to maintain the drinking and the cycle perpetuates itself.

As families can be characterized as falling somewhere along this continuum from enmeshed, to clear, to disengaged, each family has the potential for a multitude of varying boundaries manifested in itself. Let us return to the example of an alcohol abusing father, dry spouse, and the three children.

In the following structure we see the family presented with boundaries as perceived. The mother and father are disengaged and have only sparse contact, as represented by the solid line. Mother and the first and thirdborn child are enmeshed, or stuck together, in an overly close dysfunctional relationship, dysfunctional in the sense that these two children are not allowed to be

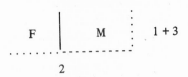

children and develop autonomy. The relationship is symbiotic and stultifying to all involved. It is common to observe the nonalcoholic spouse in a relationship with at least one youngster who has been parentified, i.e. pulled into an adult relationship and expected to satisfy needs and roles for the adult that are generally confined to the adult subsystem. The secondborn child has been able to evolve a more functional relationship with his mother, as represented by the hyphenated line (clear boundaries), while involved in an enmeshed relationship (dotted line) with father.

In this family it is likely that the mother and first and thirdborn children are in a coalition against father while the secondborn, having clear boundaries with mother, has entered an alliance with father. Assuming these boundaries are relatively stable, a problem exists in that generational boundaries have been crossed. The two children are involved with mother in roles and need satisfaction usually ascribed to the adults. Haley (1976) has commented that whenever generational boundaries are consistently violated, and members of one generation supply what should be received in another generation, pathology can be expected.

Naturally treatment concerns begin to become evident from a quick observation of this family. One concern is that of facilitating all of the children being together as a sibling subsystem and the same being true for the adults in a parental/marital subsystem. A functional goal would also be that of trying to develop clear boundaries between all of the subsystems involved. While this may be the ultimate goal, we must remember that to move too quickly will upset the current family homeostasis and probably amplify the family's resistance to change. It is as though attempting change too quickly induces too much stress and threat, and it is only natural to expect increased defensiveness.

SYMPTOMS

In the system framework, symptoms are regarded as existing to fill some function in the family. Even though the symptom may be perceived as one stimulating much distress and psychological turmoil, it is thought that it is adaptive and purposeful within the system. Paolino and McCrady (1977) have offered four possible roles of symptoms within a family system.

One role of symptomatology may be to assure acceptance into the family. The father who is unable to fulfill more traditional roles, such as breadwinner, may only be excused and accepted by being sick. Thus, his sickness can now be used to excuse his otherwise apparent inability. Alcoholism is one sickness that can be used in this fashion.

The stabilization and cementing of differentiated roles within the family may be another role of the symptom. A couple who seems unable to decide how to define the control of their relationship may discover that sickness is one resolution. As one becomes alcoholic, the issue of relationship control is resolved due to the inability of the alcoholic to continue to compete. This raises the interesting question: Who is really in control? Is it the nonalcoholic spouse who overtly appears to be in control? Is it the alcoholic who, through the symptom, forces the other to take control and is, therefore, the ultimate controller?

The third role of a symptom, as offered by Paolino and McCrady, is that of serving as a signal of stress or strain in the system. Assume the system was functioning quite well until an adaptation is required, such as a move, new job, or birth of a child. The old rules and roles are no longer effective, and the family does not have a rule regarding how rules can be changed; this results in family stress. At this time, one member of the family begins to abuse chemicals as a means of acting out the stress and signaling that something needs to be done.

The last possible role of a symptom in the family is that of a responsibility avoiding maneuver. If I get drunk and express hostility towards my wife, but yet make it obvious that I am drunk, I can cripple my wife regarding her responses to me. While I hurt my wife, for her to gain retribution may induce guilt because of my "obviously" incapacitated state. As she is left with relatively few alternatives, she is rendered relatively impotent and out of control of the situation and relationship.

While searching for the cause of the symptom can be interesting and almost border on becoming a parlor game, the important consideration is that symptoms are often messengers of more pervasive relationship issues. To effect the most efficient and long-lasting treatment effects, it is deemed advisable to treat the system or context in which the system is found. This seems to be the important learning to be acquired from perceiving behavior as symptoms.

COMMUNICATION

"Communication, verbal or nonverbal, is the vehicle through which family members touch each other and regulate their emotional closeness or distance. Every interaction between two or more family members involves not only the sharing of information, but also the shaping and determining of the relationship's involved" (Barnard and Corrales, 1979, p. 172). Along with these characteristics of family communication, this is also the most overt and observable of the various elements of family systems described in this chapter. Communication is also the vehicle through which the other elements, previously described in this chapter, are most strongly presented and shaped.

What's to Be Learned

Through analysis of a family's communication patterns much can be learned about the roles (Who is the decision maker? Who is the disciplinarian?), rules (How are decisions made? How can feelings be expressed and to whom?), prominence of homeostasis (As efforts are made to define someone as something, other than an alcoholic, do others disrupt the process or vehemently protest?), boundaries (Who talks with whom, and in what way is the relationship defined by how they communicate with one another?), and symptoms (What is it that is described as the problem(s) as compared to what seem to be more pervasive and destructive issues?). It seems obvious that a wealth of information about the family can be gathered by the therapist who is sensitive to communication patterns and styles. For this reason, the therapist as stimulator and observer of the family's communication pattern is of primary importance to efficient and effective treatment.

Two Common Communication Dysfunctions

As we think about families and how they communicate, it seems there are two general dysfunctions to which one should be sensitive. One is the potential for becoming so lost in the content of the message that awareness of the process patterns is lost. The other consists of over-attending to the process and thereby not achieving closure on specific content issues. Both of these carry tremendous potential for stimulating frustration, and just as the family can get caught up in either, so can the therapist.

To become so engrossed in determining how much was drunk, and how often, can be particularly damaging to couples. This is a common content issue presented in alcoholic families. It will thus be used as an illustration of becoming stuck in content. One person is generally only responding to how the other is saying whatever he is saying, and the interaction quickly spirals into an attack/defend process and becomes counterproductive. If the therapist gets caught up in this, he soon finds himself as immobilized and ineffective in the relationship as the couple. On the other hand, the therapist can get so caught up in the process (how they are communicating—styles, patterns, etc.) that important content issues in need of resolution are never brought to a negotiated closure.

The therapist's task consists of identifying when the process is resulting in counterproductive work and judiciously intervening to facilitate the development of a more productive direction. Gerald Zuk describes what he refers to as the "go-between role or process" as an effective means of completing this task. "It's a role in which you mediate exchanges among the members of the family; you try to facilitate meaningful exchanges among the people. At the same time you can interpret, but the interpretation level and direction and focus is hinged to your notion of where these people are and their readiness to hear certain types of information" (Zuk, 1975, p. 58). As the couple's process begins to escalate, the therapist intervenes to temporarily "short-circuit" their communication and redirect them in a more productive style.

Just as therapists must tend to the family's process, so must there be attention to the content issues. A common piece of content, in working with alcoholic families, is the poor sexual relationship between the spouses. One example of the prominence of this issue is found in the study by Strack and Dutton (1971) regarding participants in an alcoholic treatment program. They found that whether male or female, alcoholic or nonalcoholic spouse, *all* reported feelings of sexual inadequacy and failure. We also know that prolonged and severe use of alcohol can actually result in permanent sexual impotence, even if sobriety is achieved (Lemere and Smith, 1973). Considering these points, it should come as no surprise that sexuality will be a frequent content issue in the treatment process. As prominent as this is, it is not uncommon to find it to be a difficult content issue to facilitate constructive communication around. This writer's experience suggests that the spouse who regards self as least "responsible" for the sexual problems attempts to introject it as an issue and is then frequently challenged by the other spouse in order to prohibit the development of discussion. The challenge may come through an attempted disqualification such as: "Is that all you think of?" or "If you weren't such a pervert!" Often the challenge will be issued in a more indirect fashion, such as the one spouse pretending the other's comment on sex was not heard and commencing an assault about some other unrelated issue. This diversionary tactic cannot be allowed to continue too long without interruption by the therapist or soon both spouses will think that the therapist is as uncomfortable with sex as they are. Sexual expression between the couple can be a valuable tool to facilitate their "reconstruction," and as suggested, in most cases this content issue must be confronted in order to develop new behaviors and eliminate old myths and unrealistic expectations. Naturally, this discussion of sexuality is simply used as an illustration of one content issue that seems essential to be negotiated by the couple. As intriguing as working with a family's process can be, we must not lose sight of the content issues that are in need of a negotiated understanding and closure.

Congruence

Jerry Lewis, in his excellent book designed to be used by

families, describes families in which clearness of communication is confounded by, among other things, lack of congruence: "Other families, however, are very obscure, and the observer may feel either that the family is using some type of undecipherable shorthand or that the level of disorganization makes much of what they say hard to understand" (Lewis, 1979, p. 57). When around a person or persons who are incongruent, it is easy to find one's self feeling particularly confused, frustrated, and at times bordering on insanity.

Congruence refers to agreement or coordination of all levels of a message. Naturally, incongruence refers to that phenomena of mixed or contradictory messages being sent simultaneously or in such a fashion that confusion results for the receiver. The matter of congruency of communication is a particularly important one in working with alcoholic families. The history of their relationships is probably heavily checkered with deception of and by both partners. A great deal of attention must be devoted to developing congruency in their treatment process. This author's experience with alcoholic families suggests that there is often confused and contradictory messages sent regarding what they perceive in or about one another, what they are feeling, what they are thinking, and what they would like to do about various issues and situations. While working with alcoholic families on enhancing congruency of their communication can be very tedious work, the rewards for the family are well worth the effort. By changing this element of the communication process, tremendous concomitant changes will often be observed. Richard Bandler, John Grinder, and Virginia Satir have said: "In our work, we have found that assisting family members in having new choices at the process level in any area of content will generalize naturally to other areas of their experience" (Bandler, Grinder, and Satir, 1976, p. 97).

SUMMARY

At the outset of this chapter, mention was made of the family therapist's concern with the what and how dimensions of the family, as opposed to the why. This chapter has identified a number of variables that are of importance to the therapist working with alcoholic families. The chapter to follow will illustrate the manner in which these variables are operationalized into active treatment.

Chapter 3

TREATMENT FROM THE
FAMILY PERSPECTIVE

INTRODUCTION

The susceptible individual drinks, develops primary psychological dependence which is translated clinically into craving,
develops physical dependence which produces loss of control, is
caught in the vicious addictive cycle, and becomes an alcoholic
(Kissin, 1977, p. 9).

J UST as this cycle develops with considerable predictability,
there is equal certainty that the cycle must be broken for
recovery to proceed. Depending upon where on the continuum
the individual is in progression from social drinker, to heavy
drinker, to problem drinker, to early alcoholic, to moderate
alcoholic, to severe alcoholic, the need for various intervention
modalities is determined. Certainly, if physical addiction is
present, there will be the need for detoxification and then a half-
or three-quarter way living environment as the recovery and
transition proceeds. Just as this is one possibility, there may also
not be the need for detoxification and inpatient or halfway house
placement, but rather total outpatient care. Regardless of what
point the individual is at on the continuum, it seems to this writer
that the family should become engaged in the treatment process
as soon as possible.

As the opening quote of this chapter describes the destructive
cycle of alcoholism, there is another vicious cycle that must be
upset: that cycle in which the family is caught. This writer has yet
to see a family in which alcoholism was prominent where

patterns of a destructive nature were not also prominent. Many who have gone through treatment have identified the prominence of these patterns, with dismay, when they refer to their thoughts that sobriety was perceived as what was needed to change the family situation but instead seemed to amplify the discomfort present in the family relationships. This realization, without proper intervention and understanding, can be one of the primary determinants in the resumption of drinking. It is as though another illusion has been destroyed, as the alcoholic's tolerance for frustration has not been sufficiently enhanced yet to be resilient to this "shock." Without appropriate "shock absorbers," it is unrealistic to expect the individual to maintain sobriety, and the installation of these "shock absorbers" should be the focus of early treatment. AA has capitalized on this "shock absorber" concept in ways such as the sponsor arrangement, frequency of meetings, and availability of publications designed to help people through the transition via understanding and support.

In a fashion similar to AA, this writer believes the early involvement of the family in treatment can begin to facilitate all of the members assuming more of a shock absorber status with one another, as opposed to mutual destruction. The negative, destructive cycle can begin to evolve into a more benevolent and constructive cycle, which serves to instill hope, which has such tremendous curative power in and of itself. The element of hope is also a dimension of the human experience which, to varying degrees, has not been very prominently sensed by the family members for some time.

BEGINNING

As mentioned in Chapter 1, the potential for synergism of family therapy with AA seems obvious. The two are potentially very complementary, and workers in both fields should be continually aware of the advisability of coorperation with the other. Ideally, the alcoholic counselor would involve a family therapist as early as possible in the treatment process and vice versa with the family therapist where alcoholism is prominently mentioned in work with a couple or family. It is only through this awareness and resultant cooperation that the client unit can most effectively and efficiently be helped.

WHO IS PRESENT?

Just as there is the need for the professionals to have this mutual awareness and appreciation of one another, this also seems to be an appropriate place to start with the family of the abuser/alcoholic and the individual. The first session ideally should consist of all members of the family to gather their perceptions of the family situation and begin to discuss the potential for change and the role of all involved in the change process.

The value of having all members present cannot be overestimated. In all probability, at least one family member, and more than likely a greater number, have felt unimportant or discounted in relation to the family. The urgent request for all to be present communicates the message that all are valued and viewed as being part of the current family situation and pathway to change. Children and others who were not involved from the beginning perceived themselves as only observers once they were invited into the sessions. Not only is this a debilitating perception for them to possess, but time is then required to counter this perception and convince them of the important role they occupy in the therapeutic process. Especially in the early stages of treatment, all the available time needs to be focused on direct, active change efforts as opposed to engaging people, which could be avoided by their initial involvement.

Children seem to be viewed by many who are involved in alcoholism treatment as a primary means of inducing guilt and/or shame with the alcoholic. This is unnecessary, often counterproductive, and potentially destructive to the children. For many individuals, the heightening of guilt and/or shame may do nothing more than stimulate further drinking, acting out the guilt in the form of hostility, or perhaps even a suicide attempt. The children used in this fashion are also particularly vulnerable to manipulation by adults and, once manipulated into making certain statements, become overwhelmed by guilt and remorse themselves. There seems to be more productivity in involving the children in the treatment process as possessors of perceptions and desires for change as opposed to "levers for guilt."

The children's presence also provides the worker the potential for observing many dynamics of the family in need of change that would otherwise be unavailable. It must also be remembered that there is only one opportunity for observing the family when they are all equal strangers to the involved professional. If I see only the spouses and then have them bring the children with them the second time, the children are the only ones who perceive themselves as strangers in this session.

Along with the person who will work with the whole family, it is wise to have the alcoholism counselor present, assuming these will be two separate individuals. In this fashion all can use this session to arrive at an understanding of the roles all will assume and clarify ground rules for operation such as: both counselors will be in frequent contact with one another; information gained in any phone calls to either worker, placed between sessions, can be shared with all involved at the discretion of the worker; and, what are the consequences of behavior such as resumed drinking or missed sessions. Certainly the professionals involved need to demonstrate a respect for one another and a stability that discourages the client unit from temptation to triangle them, or "divide and conquer."

WHAT TO OBSERVE

In this first session, with all present, there is a need to acknowledge involvement of all and the need for everyone's involvement in the change process. An analogy of a suspended mobile has proven to be valuable for communicating this concept to families (by indicating that a mobile hanging from the ceiling has many parts to it, but that pulling on any one part activates all the others is similar to what happens in families). If one family member is distressed, troubled, acting out, or dysfunctional, it will ripple out and affect all the others. Continuing by communicating—that it is this sense of connectedness and involvement that makes it valuable for all to be involved—has proven to be effective. Once this initial rationale for everyone's involvement is established, it is time to begin to move and observe.

MAKING CONTACT

Shapiro has stated: "It is imperative that the therapist come to know each family member and his/her contribution to the overall system of relationships. It is also a necessary precondition of treatment that rapport be established with all family members, and this can best be achieved through an empathic understanding of the unique personality and characteristic role behavior of each" (Shapiro, 1977, p. 71-72). This latter point of Shapiro's statement is essential to keep in mind. If I do not take time to establish rapport with each member and make contact with them, there is the risk that they will activate their resistances to further involvement, feel unimportant and devalued, and perhaps leave them with the perception that the only way to be attended to is through acting out. It is particularly easy to fall into the trap of communicating only with the older individuals who are "logical" and "intelligent," or those who are most ready to speak. The therapist who avoids the opportunity to spend time with particularly young children is also passing up a rich opportunity for not only engaging the children into the therapeutic process, but the parents as well. Regardless of how dastardly the parent may be perceived as, this writer has yet to meet the parent who did not respond favorably to the individual who is interested, concerned, and considerate of the parent's children. This is a rich source for cementing a therapeutic relationship that is often neglected.

A benign question, such as "what's it like for you in this family?" can be a convenient way of beginning which not only provides information, but facilitates contact with each person in the family. Starting with the children is necessary in order to avoid their statements being determined by what the parents have said initially, and especially the nonalcoholic spouse. A frequent occurrence is for one of the parents to attempt to "correct" what the children are saying or embellish it. This needs to be discouraged and can be done so by simply saying to the parent that their concern is appreciated but they will have their own chance, and that it is important for everyone to have their own chance to say what they want. This intervention not only interrupts a probable pattern of the parent(s) speaking for the children, but also communicates to all present that everyone is valued here. This also may be the first time the therapist has the opportunity to directly demonstrate how he/she is able to affect the family in a way that results in their being different from that to which they are accustomed. This intervention is one the writer refers to as being designed to "eliminate the noise." Frequent interruptions, in the form of corrections, attacks, loud sighs, etc., must be dealt with so that the chaos, which has probably characterized the family, can begin to be replaced by order. With extremely disruptive families, the author has utilized a procedure that has proven particularly useful as an "eliminator of noise." A piece of paper is taken and rolled into a ball and then introduced to the family as the token that entitles whoever possesses it to talk. This rule is true for all but the therapist. This procedure has also provided other information: how do they get it from one another; who gives it to each other person most quickly/slowly; who is skipped or allowed least access to it; and when the paper is removed by the therapist does its effect seem to have generalized?

DEALING WITH DISCUSSION OF ALCOHOL-RELATED BEHAVIOR

At this juncture it can be easy to allow the family, especially the nonalcoholic spouse, to spend considerable time talking about the alcoholic's behavior, rich with historical anecdotes. This is important to short circuit in order to prevent the family from focusing-in on what is already too familiar to the detriment of what might be considered for change. The therapist is also wise to be sensitive to such characteristics as the alcoholic's sensitivity to criticism and proclivity for denial. Criticism or a judgmental attitude are sure to activate these characteristics. The therapist should be striving for a consistently benign, non-judgmental attitude to pervade the therapeutic setting. Intentions of "changing" the alcoholic will reflect a rescuing attitude and promote the proverbial power struggle, which is probably going to eventuate in further drinking and simply be a replay of the dynamics that have already been acted out in the family.

Discussions that seem to evolve about the alcohol-related behaviors should be directed toward a determination of the apparent "adaptive consequences" it engendered such as those identified by Berenson (1976). As Shapiro has stated: "Specific episodes can be examined by inquiring what happened between family members preceding, during, and subsequent to the drinking. This will establish a model of regarding it as a family problem. Most important, however, it provides the therapist with an understanding of the interpersonal factors that trigger the drinking, how it is reacted to, and how it may be discouraged or reinforced by various family members" (Shapiro, 1977, p. 72). This practice will probably also force the family to begin regarding the drinking in a fashion that is geared to increased understanding and improved opportunities for responding to one another in different ways. To this point in time it is likely that discussions of drinking have been heavily laden with affect and little movement toward constructive, rational problem solving. In this sense the family's past approach to the problem has done nothing more than confound it. As Watzlawick and his associates (1974) have identified, it seems that so often human suffering comes about more as a result of selection of inadequate solutions as opposed to being precipitated by what is perceived as the "problem." The above identified means of changing the way the family talks about the alcoholic-related behavior serves to begin to introduce them to a new solution that can hopefully be more productive and less confounding than the prior nagging, criticism, and strong affect.

Another observation of the writer's is that if the "same old way" of talking about the alcohol-related behavior is not short-circuited, the family quickly becomes discouraged and is a likely candidate for termination. From their perspective it is under-standable that termination seems a reasonable alternative. After all, for what reason should they upset schedules to make appointments, pay a fee, and risk the potential of greater pain if all that happens in the session is the same thing that occurs at home, i.e. nagging, attacking, or defending. Before moving on, it seems important to emphasize the importance of not allowing singular focus on the drinking and making what discussion there is more purposive. This can be done through focusing on apparent adaptive consequences as well as a statement such as "OK, we all know Dad has a problem with his drinking and he'll be working with John (therapist) about that, but what about other elements of the family you would like changed?''

BOUNDARIES AND ALLIANCES

Boundaries, as discussed in Chapter 2, can begin to be determined in this first session. Immediately, upon everyone seating themselves in the consultation room, a quick glance will determine who is closest/most distant from the others. This can serve as one reflection of family boundaries. Observance of family interaction will also communicate who can speak to whom and in what ways. The mother who sits with one child snuggled up next to her, and who is obviously protective of the child's territory being invaded in any way, is probably reflective of a fused or enmeshed relationship. Whereas in this same family it seems apparent that mother and father find it extremely difficult to even look at one another, let alone talk, a safe assumption is that their relationship can be characterized as disengaged. It is then noticed that the middle child and mother can interact quite candidly and share the spectrum of feelings and thoughts. This latter relationship seems to be able to be identified as having clear boundaries.

As I give consideration to the boundaries that characterize this relationship, it is a small step to consider the possibility of alliances within the family structure. What subgroups do there appear to be in this family and about what do they ally with one another? I may note that the mother and the oldest child appear to be in alliance when discussion of the consequences of drinking proceed. At the same time, father and the youngest child have an opposing view to mother and oldest, while the middle child maintains a neutral posture in relation to both of the alliances. Perhaps the alliances change, or else seem more prominent or perhaps even potentially destructive, with the advent of a new issue.

Both boundaries and alliances can begin to be intervened with at this point, but naturally in a sensitive fashion. An appropriate intervention may be nothing more than reporting the observation to the family and asking them if they had noticed it before. Perhaps moving further seems appropriate, so they are asked to discuss this observation and what they believe are the consequences of what is being reported for their family. A further extension may be that of encouraging them to reverse roles and continue with a dialogue. For instance, mother and the oldest child would switch roles with the alliance represented by father and the youngest child and proceed to talk. It is important to follow an activity such as this role reversal with a time for discussion of how it was for them. This activity can give a quick assessment of how well they do seem to understand one another as they extend efforts to represent the other(s).

Physical movement may also be a good way of acting upon the perceived boundaries and family structure. It may be noted that there is one or more children sitting between the parents. Not only does this seem to reflect the way the family is structured outside of the sessions, but it makes it more difficult for mother and father to communicate directly. An effective move may be to ask the father, or mother, to change seats with the children so s/he is next to the spouse. This, without verbal explanation, serves to graphically portray the generational boundary and the two separate subsystems of parents and children. This can be further accentuated by the therapists' placement of self between the parents as one group and the children as the other.

Another means of both assessing and beginning to effect change in the area of boundaries and alliances is through utilization of the Family Bond Inventory (Fullmer, 1972). This very simple, but powerful, procedure quickly portrays how the individuals perceive the relationships in the family with regards to boundaries and alliances. All that is needed are pencils and 8½ by 11 typing paper. Each person is given a pencil and piece of paper and then the following directions are given. "I would like to have each of you imagine the paper in front of you is a room you are suspended above. As you look down on this room, with no furniture in it, imagine all your family is in there and can move about until each individual comes to a place they are comfortable at. Use a circle to represent each person, then place their initial in the circle. It is important that you remember that this is a room without any furniture and that none of you have ever been in this room before. Are there any questions before you begin?"

After each individual has completed their representation of the family members, each in turn presents their production to the rest of the family along with their explanation regarding placement of the members. This way, it is the family doing the interpreting and not the therapist. It has proven valuable to ask questions of the family such as: "Whose production most surprises you?;" "Whose were you least surprised by;" and "This seems to suggest how each of you currently sees your family. How would you like your family to be? Would you make another now?" This last directive gets at their "ideal" and acknowledges their initial production as the "actual," or how they experience the family now.

Circle size on the Family Bond Inventory (FBI) seems to reflect the power the individual perceives each member as possessing. When the FBI was standardized, it was determined that on 8½ by 11 paper the average circle size was one-half inch. The larger the circle, the greater the perceived power possessed by the person the circle represents. The smaller the circle the less the power possessed. Again, on 8½ by 11 paper distances of less than 1 inch between circles represents fused relationships and probably an alliance. When there are 3½ inches or greater between the circles, it can be assumed that the relationship is disengaged, with little contact and probably a schism. In the initial standardization it was determined that distances between circles of 1½ to 3 inches represented a relationship probably best characterized as having clear boundaries.

The FBI, while only taking a few minutes to complete, can provide valuable information to not only the therapist, but the family members as well. It is a procedure that can be used as often as desired, and the author has used it not only for initial diagnosis and treatment planning (goal setting) with the family, but also for evaluation as the sessions progress. It seems to provide families that are not accustomed to thinking or talking about how they are, an excellent stimulus and model. Naturally this is particularly appropriate for most families where alcoholism is an issue.

Therapeutic action can be initiated through utilization of the FBI quite readily. As each individual presents their representation they are asked which relationship they would most like to change between themselves and someone else in the family. After this is identified, they are asked what they could and would do in an effort to begin initiating that change. As a result of this interaction, the format for change begins to be crystallized. One step further can be made by asking the involved to negotiate an agreement for change right now and identify it as a task to be begun that will be checked on in the next session.

In the following structure the reader will find a representation of an FBI that is characteristic of so many families with alcoholism. Assuming an alcoholic father, mother, and three children, one can quickly discern the alliance between mother and the oldest and youngest child who are at some distance (disengaged) from the father. The middle, or second, child is between the father and mother—first and third child alliance and probably functioning as the "switchboard" between these subsystems of the family. You might also note the reduced size of fathers circle and lower placement on the paper, all suggestive of a perceived reduction in power. The increased size of the oldest child's circle represents the perceived greater power possessed. A safe guess may be that this portrayal was made by the youngest daughter who perceives the oldest sibling as a powerful parent. So often this is the case, as the father and mother are caught up and almost debilitated by involvement and preoccupation with the drinking. The oldest sibling then becomes involved in "parentification" (see Chapter 2) and assumes an overfunctional role. This is not, of course, an age appropriate role for one of the youngsters and one in need of change as therapy progresses.

ROLES AND RULES

In the process of maintaining the family's homeostasis or equilibrium, people assume and are delegated to certain roles. The more dysfunctional the family, the more calcified people are into these roles. In more functional families, the individuals have the potential for occupying various roles, and they will not be relegated to just one, or a few at best, in order to maintain the family's stability. As families become more functional, there is a concomitant growth in the potential and flexibility of roles assumed.

For many years the nonalcoholic spouse has been identified as assuming the role of martyr, which certainly facilitates the enabling of the drinking, though the drinking serves to facilitate

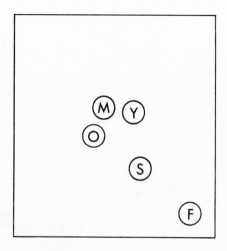

M = Mother
Y = Youngest Child
O = Oldest Child
S = Second Child
F = Father

the maintenance of the martyr role as well. The drinker serves in the role of patient, and it is difficult to have a patient without the enabling martyr and vice versa. Whalen (1953) identified the following four roles as being characteristic of wives of alcoholics: "Suffering Susan," "Controlling Catherine," "Wavering Winifred," and "Punitive Polly." A presumption of Whalen's was that these women married alcoholics in order to live out their roles. Today there is a greater attempt to understand how family members reciprocally assume and delegate roles within the system framework; one then intervenes to short-circuit the narrowness and rigidity that the roles confer.

Roles common to children in alcoholic families are the "lost child," the "mascot," and "little adult," and others. The firm acceptance of these roles within the family, and likelihood of the youngster generalizing the role appropriate behavior to the peer group, is counterproductive to children fully developing their potential. The "lost child," for instance, becomes aloof and withdrawn from the others. This child is likely to be overweight and rejecting, perhaps as a means of defending from being rejected first. The "lost child's" internal affective experience is likely to be feelings of inadequacy, loneliness, hurt, and anger. The "mascot," likely to be the youngest child, is characterized by attention-getting behaviors such as "being cute," fragile, physically ill, and/or infantilized. The "little adult," the child who is most parentified (see Chapter 2), is the one who is super responsible, "old beyond their years," "mother's helper," the "good kid." This role makes it very difficult for the youngster to indeed be a "kid" and go through the necessary developmental stages of growing up. This child is probably without many friends and a source of support in the peer group, due to the over-involvement in the home and regarding peer group activities as childish. Roles such as these need to be identified and efforts made to begin introducing flexibility into who can assume them and opening the family to the realization of the many other alternative roles all might assume. This can many times be initiated by assigning the role and encouraging the normal occupant to take a "vacation" this week and try out a new role that can be negotiated within the session. As various family members are assigned new roles for the period between sessions they are encouraged to have fun with them. Upon their return to the next session, a quick go-around of grading can be completed as a means of soliciting feedback. In the go-around, everyone is encouraged to assign a grade to each individual for their performance in their selected/delegated role during the past week. While this can be made into a light-hearted activity, it is also a means of introducing the family to a feedback process. While "light-hearted" may be frowned at by some, this writer believes that for most families with alcoholism present in them, light-hearted activities have been few and far between and any activity of this nature can be helpful to the family. The value of laughing and having fun together should never be underestimated in favor of the illusion that treatment always needs to be "heavy" in order to be effective.

Closely aligned with roles are family rules. Dodson and Kurpius (1977) have given examples of many family rules: How and when may one let needs and wants be known to another; When and how may one respond to the needs and wants of others; How may one gain self-esteem and how much may one have;

How may one grow and change in another's presence; How may
one be a man or a women and a human being; How may one feel
and express sexuality; Who can talk to whom; About what may
one speak; What, when and how may one comment on what one
sees, feels, and thinks; How may one show feelings such as love,
hurt, and anger; How may one receive those feelings from
another; and, When and how may a member go away from this
family to relate to others?

While these questions are used here to identify varying rules
that are operational in families, these same questions can be
posed directly to families. Through confrontation of one family
with these questions, the therapist can learn about the family as
the family learns new ways of thinking about how they operate as
a social system. While these rules are the skeleton of the family's
system, they are frequently outside of the family's awareness and
are implied rather than explicit. Once the family members
become aware of their rules, choices become more feasible and the
potential is increased for them to participate more consciously in
developing more facilitative rules.

COMMUNICATION NUANCES

Every interaction between two or more family members
involves not only the sharing of information, but also the
shaping and determining of the relationship involved. The
information shared, or *report* component of the message, is what
the words together mean as defined by a dictionary. The shaping
component, or *relationship* part of the message, is conveyed via
the vocal and linguistic patterns utilized in conjunction with the
bodily gestures and context in which the message is shared. Most
people have enough common sense to realize that "how"
something is said is in most cases at least as important as what is
said. This becomes particularly true in families where alcoholism
has been present. There is more likely a history of unpleasant
experiences and concomitant negative feelings. With this history
it is not unusual to come to the realization that various family
members have become an aversive stimulus to one another in the
classical sense of the word. The wife looks and/or hears the
husband and finds herself overwhelmed with negative feelings
from the past, regardless of how or what he is now saying. Her

response is then shaped more by these negative feelings than in reaction to how and what he is speaking now. The husband feels discounted and reverts to counterattacking behaviors, and the two of them are right back into their old and familiar destructive styles and patterns.

Because of this it is essential for the individual working with these families to be prepared to actively intervene to short-circuit these patterns quickly. This is especially true initially, in order to demonstrate to the family that at least in these sessions they can be different. As quickly as the therapist detects family members reacting to the relationship component of the message and disregarding the report component, he must stop the process. The following are a few means by which the therapist can intervene to defuse this process. Pursuing a "shared meaning" (Miller, Nunnally, and Wackman, 1975) whereby the person receiving the message is asked to repeat (to the satisfaction of the sender) the message just received can be very effective. This procedure serves to keep the focus on the report or content component of the message, rather than encouraging the participants to just respond to the relationship component of the message. This can promote the family members negotiating an issue to closure, or at least further understanding, than what has been characteristic of how they react to one another. Another intervention consists of pointing out the process that appears to be destructive. For instance, the look on the face and/or sound and velocity of the voice that accompanied the report may be commented on. This tends to underscore the way in which the two levels of communication—report and relationship—can be incongruent or inconsistent, and confusing at best. Once the two components of the message are identified, the sender can identify which it is they choose to receive. The pathway is now open for a more logical communication process to be implemented and the probability of understanding being achieved is now increased. This writer has also found asking the family members who are attempting to communicate to turn their chairs back-to-back to be a valuable aid. When facing back to back the visual access to one another is diminished and they become more reliant upon their auditory channel and the resultant need to "listen closer" can be capitalized upon. It seems that so often those family members are so stimulated by that "certain look" that accompanies the words from the other that they react to the look and disregard the report component of the message. The effect of having them sit back-to-back can be intensified by combining it with the shared meaning approach just discussed. While initially frustrating to them because of the pressure this puts on them for changing old patterns, it can be extremely powerful. The writer has found it useful to predict that they will find this difficult and disconcerting, before they are directed to do it, to effectively neuter their attempts to short circuit this procedure by complaints such as "this is ridiculous," or "there's no sense to this." By predicting they will find it difficult and/or frustrating it makes it needless or useless for them to make similar comments. It probably also gives them relief from the social pressure they may otherwise feel as they engage clumisily in new behaviors. "Mind reading" is a common occurrence in these families. Mind reading being defined as the process of one family member attributing certain feelings, thoughts, behaviors, etc. to another member without any clear reason for the same—An example of this would be the wife who says to the alcoholic husband: "I know you never listen to me or do you care to. I may as well talk to the wall!" In this statement, she is attributing to the husband—"you never listen . . . or care to"—not only the behavior of not listening, but the feeling of not caring to listen. A quick way of confronting this mind reading would be to ask the husband what he just heard her say. Assuming he can repeat what she has communicated, the desired effect of her realizing that the mind reading is inappropriate has been implemented. In this same message of the wife's, she has also engaged in a generalization; this needs to be confronted, particularly if generalizations are a prominent part of her communication style. The generalization in this message is the word *never*. It is rare indeed that such encompassing words can be legitimately used in reference to human behavior. She has also inserted an implicit disqualification, or "put-down," by comparing her husband's ability to listen to that of a wall. Certainly it is likely that this is not going to be conducive to promoting more positive and facilitative feelings between them.

While elements of their communication process must be changed and moderated, there is a need for sensitivity in intervening. Without some caution, it seems obvious that intervention here could result in the wife feeling "put-down"; it could also result in promoting defensiveness on her part. This defensiveness then results in her turning a deaf ear to the therapist's message for her, as well as further separation between herself, the therapist, and the therapeutic process. Especially in the initial stages of treatment, until all members are engaged and fully aware that the therapist is concerned for the well-being of each of them, this writer believes these interventions need to be accompanied by a "shock absorber." Let us consider two different possible dialogues in this situation. Wife will be represented by a **W**; husband by an **H**; and the therapist by a **T**.

> **W** — I know you never listen to me or do you care to. I may as well talk to the wall!
>
> **T** — Ralph what did you just hear her say?
>
> **H** — She said I never listen to her, that I don't care to and that she may as well talk to the wall.
>
> **T** — (to wife) Well, it seems like what you have just said is not true.
>
> **W** — Here we go again. Another one who's going to take his side. He can manipulate everyone.

Note how the confrontation of the false attribution in her statement results in increased defensiveness and her reverting to almost the identical style and pattern of communication, via generalizing and mind reading, in response to the therapists' response. Certainly the likelihood of change occurring has not been enhanced.

Here is another example, only this time the confrontation is accompanied by a "shock absorber." Another way of understanding this "shock absorber" concept is via the analogy Whitaker (1967) has developed between therapy and surgery. Prior to cutting, as part of the surgery, the physician utilizes an anesthetic. In the same sense the effective family therapist judiciously utilizes an "anesthetic" before intervening strategically.

> **W** — I know you never listen to me or do you care to. I may as well talk to the wall!
>
> **T** — Ralph what did you just hear her say?
>
> **H** — She said I never listen to her—that I don't care to and that she may as well talk to the wall.

Therapist to Alice: You know, I can understand you being very frustrated after this many years of tension between you two, but it seems there may be some things you two do that make it difficult to make the relationship different. I think we just heard an example here of a broad, sweeping statement that makes it difficult for you two to get together. I'm sure Ralph does the same thing as well, with the same damaging effect. Do you hear and understand what I am saying? (I have tried to apply the anesthetic here via attributing the same behaviors to her husband. I do this with considerable assuredness, realizing that there are very few of us who can legitimately say we have never done this. I also say it in a calm, understanding way, while avoiding a condescending or placating style. My tone of voice, and style of communicating, is designed to "lend" her, or model, a different style of communicating, with the hoped for effect of her imitating me. Bandler and Grinder have written extensively on this process and the one I will mention now (1975a, 1975b, 1976, 1977). I also apply anesthetic by utilizing the sensory channel of hearing, which seems so important to her by saying Ralph never *listens* to her and that she may as well "talk to the wall." I use this channel by ending my statement with "do you *hear* and understand what I am *saying?*")

    W — Yes, and it does make sense to me. We both do it more than what we should. (She has accepted my confrontation, even though it is more comfortable for her to share it with her husband, the desired effect has been implemented.)

    T — Could you tell me how you know when Ralph is, or is not, listening to you? (I begin to move this from a name calling interaction to one of action, which is more likely to provide information leading to understanding that could be facilitative for the relationship.)

In this last example, the destructive communication pattern has been short-circuited, and the couple is being moved into an area of exploration with much more positive potential for their relationship than a continuation of their old calibrated patterns. The communication process that resides between them is slowly beginning to be changed, or at least its likelihood of occurring is increased.

In the area of communication many worthwhile assignments

can be developed for a couple/family to utilize between sessions. These assignments serve to: capitalize on all the hours in-between sessions, which can otherwise be "dead" time; introduce continuity into the sessions; and, serve as a barometer to their interest in achieving change via either their completion or lack of.

An assignment frequently used is that of asking each family member to identify one thing they will attempt to do between now and the next session to change the way the family communicates with one another. Though it is important to not be too grandiose and all encompassing, encourage them to just select one person and identify one behavior they can change. So rather than allowing, or encouraging, one person to identify one behavior they are going to change with each person, they select one person and one behavior. Typical assignments may be those such as the following, assuming a family with mother, father and three kids:

> Mother—"I will try to refrain from using my "whining" tone of voice, as we have discussed today, with my husband."
>
> Husband—"I will try to give my wife more compliments than I do, and I will start by complimenting her at least three times a day on the reduction in frequency of her 'whining' tone."
>
> First Child—"I will try to not criticize my two younger brothers for their behavior by calling them names I know they don't like."
>
> Second Child—"I will speak directly to Dad rather than asking him for things through Mom."
>
> Third Child—"I will try to stop my crying whenever I don't get what I want from mother."

In conjunction with this type of assignment, it is often wise to ask them if someone in the family may be able to help them be more successful in meeting their goal, and, if so, who that is and how they might be helpful. This creates one opportunity for exchange of behaviors and them beginning to perceive one another as helpful rather than an enemy or adversary.

Another assignment that is particularly effective is to ask them to "surprise one another." After a session, or sessions, where their communication process has been worked with, ask them to "surprise one another with new communication behaviors." They are instructed not to let the others know what they are going to do, but for each person to decide upon at least one new communication behavior to practice between this and the next session. They are also told that if someone tries to identify or guess what it is they are attempting to do, they are to simply say, "remember we aren't supposed to discuss this until the next session." They are then informed that at the start of the next session they will each be encouraged to guess what each other was trying to do, and then each will disclose what it was they were attempting. This assignment has a number of purposes. It serves to allow each to select what they want to do and also gets each one to begin to be more sensitive to positive behaviors that emanate from one another. They know that each has been instructed to do something more constructive this week and that is what they are now sensitized to. This dimension of the assignment capitalizes on at least two assumptions which seem accurate in most cases: (1) people are competitive and they will want to be able to identify what the others have been trying to do in-between sessions, so as not to be "shown up" by the others; and (2) their history has probably sensitized them to being aware of the negative behaviors of one another and overlooking those behaviors that are positive. This assignment encourages them to reverse this cycle and start becoming more aware of those positive behaviors that are exchanged among them. Along with these elements, this assignment can be fun for them to engage in as they attempt to guess what the others are doing. Having fun is probably something they have not had much of together, at least in the recent past as discussed in the section of this chapter dealing with rules and roles. At the start of the next session then, each is asked to identify what they think the others were attempting to do and then each, in turn, identifies what they were indeed trying to do and what they perceived the effects as being.

Assuming the family owns a tape recorder, or one is available for them to use, the recorder can be used effectively for an assignment focusing on communication. They are asked to talk for just ten minutes a day (some request them to talk longer, but the author believes that more than ten minutes a day is too big of an order for most alcoholic families, especially initially) about whatever they want, but utilizing their newly learned skills and then record it. There are times when also asking them to talk about a specific issue or issues is effective. Depending on the family, they may be asked to talk about what makes it difficult to share feelings in the family, or what rules in the family make it most difficult for change to occur, or how the presence of the alcohol induced behavior interferes with the family, or how the alcohol induced behavior "helps" the family via expression of aggression, etc. The assigning of what is to be talked about is certainly an idiosyncratic thing to each family and the therapeutic system of themselves and the therapist(s). In most cases, the therapist does not have sufficient time to listen to the entire tape upon their return, so they can be asked to just play that portion they are most pleased about and/or that portion they believe reflects a problem area for them. This is an assignment that can be used over and over again as long as it seems productive.

Just as communication is crucial to family relationships and a potential source of much difficulty, it can also be a rich and fertile ground for the therapist to be sensitive to in helping the family to effect change. Barnard and Corrales have said: "Communication, verbal or nonverbal, is the vehicle through which family members touch each other and regulate their emotional closeness or distance" (Barnard and Corrales, 1979, p. 172). So to can communication be "the vehicle through which" families achieve therapeutic change."

SUMMARY

In this chapter the therapeutic process of effecting change in alcoholic families was examined. The principles of family operations were explored with reference to intervening in order to help the family relate in a more productive, growth-enhancing fashion. As a result of these interventions, the idea is that the alcoholism can be more quickly and effectively eliminated as a contaminating variable to family functioning and vice versa.

Dimensions of the therapeutic process with alcoholic families such as who should be present, how to start, what to observe, and how to implement change, based upon observations, were presented and discussed. While certainly not exhaustive, the chapter was designed to expose the reader to important dimensions of family intervention.

Chapter 4

THE FAMILY'S ADJUSTMENT
TO ALCOHOLISM

INTRODUCTION

A NUMBER. of publications have addressed the issue of how the family struggles to maintain itself in spite of the debilitating effects that seem to be generated by the presence of alcoholism in a member (Cohen, 1966; Rooney, 1975; Bowen, 1974; and Jackson, 1954). Anyone who has been involved with families of alcoholics is aware of the prominence of tension, fear, isolation, rejection, incongruence, blaming, denial, and inhuman rules which are operational. Perhaps Howard and Howard have captured the essence of the family's experience when they said:

> The people who live with the problem drinkers are like clocks slowly ticking, but there is no way to know whether they are going to run down and stop or are attached to explosives—time bombs ready to explode. The people who live with the problem drinker progress through a debilitating process as markedly as the alcoholic progresses through the early, middle, and late stages of alcoholism. As the condition of the problem drinker deteriorates, the family suffers through lack of or distorted communication and decreasing levels of self-worth; the family atmosphere becomes less nurturing and more disturbed (1978, p. 140).

As chaotic and disorganized as these families appear to be, there tends to be patterns of adjustment which are discernible with most families. The patterns that have been described and seem to enjoy the most widespread acceptance are those identified many years ago by Joan Jackson (1954). Even though there has been some criticism of the stages identified by Jackson, the fact remains that they have stood the test of time and not been replaced by any more apparently sound set of constructs.

THE FAMILY ADJUSTS

For purposes of more clearly understanding the family's reaction to the presence of alcoholic drinking, Jackson's stages will be discussed at this juncture. It seems important to remember, prior to discussing the stages of adjustment, that whenever one is dealing with human beings, it is vital to be continuously cognizant of the fact that there are exceptions to rules and human differences. While the stages will be presented in a linear fashion, not all families will progress in an orderly, step-by-step fashion through these stages. As tempting as it might be to organize our perceptions, and then let our experience be shaped accordingly, any experienced clinician is aware of the exceptions to "neat packages." As already mentioned, Jackson's conceptualizations provide us with a model, but must not be interpreted as meaning all families follow this identified "path" exactly.

It is also of value to be aware of Jellinek's work, which identifies the stages of deterioration in the alcoholic (Jellinek, 1960). This model of Jellinek's is more commonly referred to as the "dip chart," reflecting the progressive downward path of deterioration observed in the alcoholic before "hitting bottom" and then beginning the upward climb to wellness and reorganization. In the discussion to follow, Jackson's family stages will be related to Jellinek's stages of deterioration observed with the progressive development of alcoholism in the individual. For ease of presentation, the assumption will be made that the alcoholic is the husband, and the wife is the nonalcoholic spouse.

I. The Family Tries to Deny the Problem

In the early stages of alcoholism the alcoholic is classicly characterized as denying the prominence of the drinking. Rationalizations and an unwillingness to discuss or "belabor" the issue of drinking are observed. The drinking at this point is typically described as sporadic, excessive drinking and does result in occasional strains on the marital relationship that may become distorted and "spill over" onto the children. The alcoholic, at this point, feels resentful of being "bothered" by the nonalcoholic spouse about the drinking and then vacillates between experiencing a sense of being threatened and ashamed. These feelings can compound the drinking as the alcoholic consumes more to numb one's self from these experiences, and especially so in consideration of the inability to deal constructively with the feelings generated.

The nonalcoholic spouse minimizes the problem at this stage. She denies, similar to that of her husband, that there is a drinking problem and instead reacts to specific incidents that occur in the marriage. As she begins to feel more rejected, unloved, and unwanted, as the alcoholic becomes more preoccupied with drinking, to react against the drinking results in her feeling disloyal and seems to do little more than intensify the schism and his drinking. Her feelings of inadequacy, and resultant frustration, also mount as her efforts to please and effect change are abortive.

The children, at this stage, are probably unaware of the drinking problem but sense the tension between their parents. If the children do inquire about the drinking, they are not infrequently rebuffed, as this threatens the parents denial system. Through this process the children are taught to be "unaware" of what they observe, and the mechanism of denial is thus passed onto them.

Both employers and in-laws tend to be unaware of the drinking at this stage. Statements such as "everyone drinks" may be offered if an issue is raised regarding the drinking. Employers may even regard the drinking as useful or necessary, depending upon the type of employment. It is also not uncommon to find that many in this extra-familial circle choose not to deal with the drinking issue because it threatens them and their own drinking habits.

Friends of the couple find themselves feeling embarrassed by the behavior, which is secondary to the drinking, and the quarreling the couple engages in. They may also vacillate between feeling protective on one hand and empathetic and helpless on the other.

At this point the family is unlikely to seek out assistance. If assistance is sought it will more than likely be the nonalcoholic spouse who requests general information about alcoholism or, more typically, counseling for herself in order to resolve her marital problems without directly mentioning the drinking. In light of this last point, the author believes it is crucial to always inquire of the individual spouse seeking assistance with their marriage about the drinking practices of the spouse not present.

II. Attempts to Eliminate the Problem

In the absence of intervention, the alcoholic progresses to the crucial, or middle, phase of the three phases of alcoholic development identified by Jellinek. Characteristics of the alcoholic in this phase are dropping or losing friends, devalued personal relationships, change of family habits, decrease in sexual drive, flashes of aggression, loss of ordinary willpower, tremors and morning drinking, unreasonable resentments, intermittent periods of sobriety and/or social drinking, and all the while the excessive, out-of-control drinking increases in frequency.

While the family is aware of the serious nature of the drinking, the stigma is prominent and denial is maintained. The family makes efforts to cover up and begins to manifest the enabling behaviors of making excuses and isolating themselves. The increasing social isolation for the wife heightens her awareness and concern about the drinking and increasing marital strife. She makes attempts to solve it on her own and vacillates between excusing and pampering him as a result of her sense of guilt, anger, and attempts to counterproductively control the relationship. The more and more attention she focuses on the problem, the more angry and resentful she becomes of the apparent power the alcoholic is acquiring in her life. Feelings of self-pity, inadequacy, and guilt also accompany the anger and resentment at this stage. An obvious power struggle begins to calcify between them as she becomes as preoccupied with stopping his drinking as he is with maintaining it.

The children in this stage begin to suffer the consequences of the problems between their parents. They are exposed to the inconsistencies, confusion, and insane blend of affect that permeates the family. The alcoholic may expose them to physical and/or sexual abuse to compound their circumstances. School-related disturbances and other behavioral manifestations are evidenced by the children, which may alert sensitive people in their environment to the fact that there is disruption at home.

In-laws and employers may threaten the alcoholic or admonish him about utilizing willpower. Even though the drinking may be bothersome, behaviors such as loaning money and "giving him another chance" do nothing more than enable the further disintegration.

In this stage we also observe old friends drifting away and being replaced by the alcoholic with a new drinking crowd. The new friends remonstrate and encourage the drinking, while the nonalcoholic spouse's sense of alienation mounts. If the nonalcoholic spouse does develop new friendships, it is not uncommon to observe these friends doing little more than sympathizing with her and compounding her own sense of self-pity, helplessness, and martyrdom.

If help is sought at this stage, it is likely going to be sought for problems other than the drinking. Assistance may be requested for the children, or occasionally for the marital difficulties, without reference being made to the drinking. Middle class families often feel their status is threatened if they solicit agency assistance and thus refrain from this practice.

III. Chaos and Disorganization

The drinking of the alcoholic in this stage is frequently out of control. His life is characterized by crisis. The problems are probably a combination of economics, job difficulties, sexual frustrations, poor problem solving, and feeling victimized. Feeling victimized and wanting to avoid the accompanying pain, he maintains his drinking to anesthetize himself. The vicious cycle is now in full gear.

The wife, while perceiving her efforts as more futile than ever, continues with the same unsuccessful behaviors of nagging, hiding bottles, withholding sex, berating and chilling him with silence. She may be exposed to beatings and also begin to fear for her ability to maintain her sanity. She finds herself feeling alone, helpless, chaotic, self-loathing, and neurotic.

The children are now aware of the problem and find themselves with torn loyalties. If they align themselves with their father, they feel as though they are disloyal and rejecting their mother. The same is true if they join with their mother's recriminations of their father. They are caught in the proverbial double bind, being "damned if they do and damned if they don't." As this confusion is typically not conducive to their mental health, their problems often intensify at this stage. The author has had the experience of encountering families at this stage of adjustment as a result of an adolescent who, in his/her effort to escape the tumultuous familial situation via drugs, brings the family problem into focus. The children in this stage feel frustrated, insecure, frightened, confused and, understandably unhappy.

In-laws and employers react in often contradictory and conflicting ways. While the employer may demote or fire the alcoholic, the in-laws may loan money and bail the alcoholic out in other ways. Various in-laws may also attempt to rescue the alcoholic or other family members as sides begin to be taken. Oftentimes the behaviors are enabling and counterproductive in nature if for no other reason than the confusion that they engender.

Contact with outside agencies and services is common in this stage, but so too is withdrawal from treatment as all seems hopeless. In this stage it is also easy to perceive the nonalcoholic spouse as "neurotic," while the alcoholic is cunning enough to "con" the agency into perceiving him as being adequate and merely a victim of this "neurotic woman's ruminations." Outside intervention may also come about as a result of legal involvement at this stage, e.g. calling the police to intervene into domestic violence and/or traffic violations. Another frequently observed manifestation is that of the children acting out sufficiently to involve outside agencies. It is as though the children are sacrificing themselves in order to get help for the "craziness," which is rampant in the family at this point.

IV. Efforts to Reorganize in Spite of the Problem

The alcoholic, now into the chronic phase of Jellinek's paradigm, generally is confronted with a crisis of major proportions. The crisis may take the form of prison, or a serious accident. He may make excessive, "last ditch" efforts to regain the respect of his children via long lectures, excessive fondling, and/or beatings. At this point, it is as though he and his wife have no contact other than that which could best be characterized as bitter and resentful. He may become so confronted with the magnitude of his drinking and his inability to control it that he may opt for treatment. If he does so, and recovery is instituted, the family moves into stage VII. If not, the family progresses into Stage V.

The nonalcoholic spouse begins to organize the family alone. She manages the home, stabilizes the family, may go to work, and often seeks help for herself and the children. She no longer hides or denies the drinking problem. While she feels more positive, there are still pangs of guilt over her perceived failure. She may also feel somewhat confused about her new ascendant role and want assistance in internalizing this. Rather than reacting to the problem of alcoholic drinking, she is assuming a much more proactive stance and begins to engage in the process of "detachment" as espoused by Alanon in their work with nonalcoholic spouses. Through detaching herself, she short circuits the power struggle that she and her husband maintained for so long. It is often observed that this detachment, and resultant short circuiting of the power struggle, is what stimulates the husband into treatment and the process of recovery.

The children, beginning to feel more secure, accept that the family can re-stabilize itself and may capitalize on resources such as Alateen and/or other supportive and educational groups. While they may lose respect for the alcoholic parent they will often begin to acknowledge the concept of alcoholism as an illness in this stage. It is as though they too are better able to detach themselves from the chaos and inconsistencies that have characterized their family life.

While some in-laws pity the nonalcoholic spouse and are angered with the alcoholic, other in-laws manifest the same behaviors only to the opposite spouses. Stronger feelings may be expressed by them than at any other stage due to the obvious nature of the problem along with its chronicity. The alcoholic changes jobs of his own volition in order to escape to a new environment or is fired and moves on. The new employer is unaware of past difficulties and begins to be "conned" by the alcoholic in order for his habit to be enabled.

At this time the wife often seeks help and may become involved with Alanon as the children engage themselves with Alateen. The wife is interested in helping herself and takes this focus as opposed to expending further abortive efforts at changing the alcoholic. She may also be seeking assistance in organizing the children and herself into a new family structure in the absence of the alcoholic. These various moves may result in the alcoholic realizing that his family is moving on without him and result in his seeking treatment. If he does so, and the family decides to attempt to reorganize as a whole unit in treatment, they would progress directly to Stage VII. If he does not opt for treatment, the family will likely move to Stage V of Jackson's schema.

V. Efforts to Escape the Problem

The alcoholic in this stage feels lonely, hurt, guilty and probably extreme self-pity. The wife may leave the marriage, or he might initiate action to escape the familial environment, which serves to constantly remind him of the chaos that has racked all of them. His drinking continues to serve as an anesthetic to his feelings and simultaneously to maintain them. He is now firmly embedded in what Jellinek refers to as the chronic phase of alcoholism.

The wife leans strongly toward separation and/or divorce and feels more strongly about her growing sense of detachment. As the decision about maintenance of the marriage is more prominent, the concomitant emotional tension increases for her, but is buffered by her new found sense of strength. As she is engaged in this process, the children seem to form camps aligning themselves with mother to leave the father or else align with the father, while perceiving the mother as "unfair" for terminating the marriage.

The in-laws, by this point, may have become fairly firmly entrenched in their feelings and reactions as manifested in Stage IV. The employer may respond to the alcoholic's depression with sympathy and give him another chance.

The alcoholic may ask for reconciliation of the family and seek treatment. If not, the wife may seek assistance in making the "break" and solicit reassurance and support. She may also desire and/or be in need of specific services such as financial assistance, employment counseling, and/or general adjustment and parenting guidance. It is generally advisable to help the nonalcoholic spouse maintain her proactive, rather than reactive, posture along with providing assistance for her special needs as just identified. The children can benefit from learning about the disease concept of alcoholism at this juncture.

VI. Reorganization of Part of the Family

The alcoholic is likely to be feeling depressed, suicidal, and/or homicidal now. He is "out in the cold" as a result of separation or the actual divorce. In Jellinek's schema, he may "hit bottom" and realize all of his alibis have been exhausted and admit he is a defeated man. Unless he seeks help, the family will not progress into Stage VII, and indeed he may die or at least experience irreversible physical and/or mental damage.

The wife is reorganizing the family with herself as the head and organizes the group such that she is sustaining them. She now accepts the disease concept and probably utilizes groups such as Alanon to maintain her detachment and require assistance in managing residual guilt about deserting the alcoholic. This assistance is generally advisable, because as the disease concept of alcoholism is accepted there is often a rekindling of guilt about abandoning the "sick" husband.

The children may either reduce their acting out or intensify it in hopes of their behavior reuniting their parents. They may also be rather set in their perceptions of how things are now going to be or vacillate back and forth from one parent's side to the other's. It is the writer's experience that the children's reactions are hard to predict but do seem most predictable, and stable, if the mother and children are actively involved in treatment in order to facilitate their processing of their various concerns.

Treatment in this stage may include the nonalcoholic spouse seeking protection from the alcoholic who may be enraged at her moving away from him and establishing herself independently. The separation guilt, mentioned in Stage V, may still be presenting difficulties for her and may result in her needing futher assistance in its resolution. If the alcoholic becomes involved in treatment it is likely that he will need medical attention as well. To engage in marital counseling at this point, without the alcoholic receiving inpatient treatment for alcoholism, could be counterproductive in that it would simply help instill the delusion of their making it and then quickly falling back into the same old patterns.

VII. Recovery and Reorganization of the Whole Family

This stage is only possible if the alcoholic can assume sobriety. Dangers here are his expending efforts to "make up" for everything too rapidly, and either becoming frustrated with his inability to do it immediately, and/or his wife becoming frustrated with his over-responsibility and efforts to "control" the family. He may also project himself as being superior for "overcoming the illness" and deserving of unreasonable attention and rewards. Another risk for the recovering alcoholic is that of becoming so involved in his twelfth step work (twelfth step of the twelve suggested steps of Alcoholics Anonymous: "Having had a spiritual awakening as the result of these steps, we tried to carry this message to alcoholics, and to practice these principles in all our affairs.") that he is for all practical purposes as unavailable to his family as he was while engaged in alcoholic drinking. He may also be disillusioned, along with the rest of the family, when coming off the "treatment high." Often the alcoholic and family develop a sense of elation with treatment, which can result in them "crashing back" to reality with shocking results. All need to be cautioned about this, and the author will frequently remind families at this point that while this is a big "first step," they still have a journey to reorganization in a more functional and productive way of being.

The wife, while enthused, is also suspicious of when he might resume his drinking. She is in need of assistance in instilling a sense of trust in his capacity to maintain sobriety. Assistance will also probably be necessary in the areas of: being disillusioned with the presence of problems in the marriage in spite of sobriety being achieved; resentment over "all the help and attention" the alcoholic receives from various groups; adjusting to "make room" for the recovering alcoholic as a responsible adult and parent in the family (the author has seen families where as much as nine years after sobriety has been achieved the wife has still been unable/unwilling to "make room" for her husband to assume a responsible position in the family structure); and, once again sharing the children's attention and affection with the recovering spouse. At this point, intensive marital and family therapy is crucial to their efforts to reorganize in the most productive fashion possible and, concomittantly, to the maintenance of sobriety for the recovering spouse.

The children also have major adjustments to make. As distressing as the years of confusion may have been, the new changes may be equally distressing. There are now two competent parents to contend with, and in the process they may have lost a "special and cozy" relationship that they had with one of their parents in "the days of drinking." Not only did they find it easier to have more privileges in the "drinking days," but also they found that they were regarded more as responsible equals by at least one of the parents. Now they feel relegated to the status of child again. They may act out their discontent and/or act out in order to test the "realness" and strength of this new change.

The author can recall one such case where this occurred. A thirty-nine-year-old woman was hospitalized for depression and a suicide attempt. As the family was involved, it became apparent that the husband was drinking heavily and that the oldest daughter had been "parentified" (pulled into the adult subsystem to function as a surrogate adult for, in this case, mother [Boszormenyi-Nagy and Spark, 1973]). As the parents were worked with on their marital difficulties, and the husband with his drinking, apparently good progress was being made. All seemed to be going well until about six months later when the oldest daughter (the one who had been parentified) attempted suicide and was hospitalized. It was surprising to not only her parents, but all who had known this previously "super-responsible" adolescent. In retrospect, it was quite easy to determine that in the process of the family reorganizing, special care and attention had been given the parents and the marital relationship, but she had in essence been "relegated" to a role of child in the family without any means being made available to her to continue to feel valued and important.

While this is one specific case, the author is aware of others of a similar nature. The total family as an operational system must be acknowledged and addressed in a sensitive and aware fashion during this reorganization process. Without this type of informed treatment, negative side effects of this nature might best be expected.

Before proceeding, it seems important to once again caution the reader about overemphasizing the preceding stages of family adjustment as being immutable and always occurring in the linear fashion in which they were presented. Just as the progressive nature of alcoholism has general "bench marks," they do not always occur in the same sequence and over the same period of time with each individual. As with most of human behavior, there are individual and idiosyncratic differences that must be expected and appreciated with varying families.

DEALING WTH FAMILY DENIAL AND RESISTANCE TO TREATMENT

From the prior discussions of the stages of adjustment manifested by the family, the reader can determine that help for the problems is most often not sought until well into the process of deterioration of both the alcholic and the family. For this reason, the author believes it is essential to routinely check with clients about the pattern of drug usage by them and those in their environment. An example might be the female seeking assistance for her depression who, because of her denial and/or guilt, never acknowledges the degree to which her husband is abusing. As the treatment of her depressive state progresses, change is either very slow or nonexistent as a result of the "depressive stimulus" (her husband and his habit) not being addressed. To assume people will volunteer this information is a naive notion. As discussed in the previous section, the guilt, sense of inadequacy, denial, and sense of self-loathing all operate in a concerted fashion to make it unlikely that this concern will be shared voluntarily. This is especially true in the early stages, and naturally without an intervention the deterioration and intensity of the problem are just magnified.

There are a number of readily available brief questionnaires that can be extremely helpful in determining the degree of the drinking problem. Utilization of these tools can help clarify the problem posed by drinking as well as begin the important process of educating the nonalcoholic spouse and others about alcoholism. The process of demythologizing the drinking is extremely important at this stage. Using the Jellinek "dip chart" (1960) can be valuable as far as conveying an understanding of the progressive and predictable path of alcoholism. The "indicating signs" of alcoholism, as discussed by John Keller in the pamphlet, *Alcohol: A Family Affair* (1977), can be extremely valuable as well at this point. The twenty questions to be answered by family members, designed by Betty Reddy (1973), is similarly useful at this point. By responding to these questions the family members get immediate feedback as to the likelihood of alcoholism being manifested by one of their members. Any of these, or other similar tools, can be a valuable asset to improving the likelihood of acknowledgment of the problem, which is naturally an important and major step in the treatment process. As Howard and Howard have said regarding a questionnaire they utilize: "Answering the twenty-question questionnaire will help define the problem, determining once and for all if the drinking problem does exist. It is important for the client to have help in being able to say 'Yes, he is an alcoholic. Yes, there is a drinking problem in our family.' Breaking through denial will lay the foundation for treatment" (Howard and Howard, 1978, p. 144). This introductory educational work can also be valuable in assisting the person in developing the types of "detachment" from the alcoholic patterns, which can be so crucial in initiating change. Rather than reacting in the counterproductive fashions in which they have been, the detachment encourages them to begin to be more productively proactive.

Once the drinking problem has been established as being in existence, there is need for engaging the individual identified as alcoholic, along with the rest of the family. At this point it is often valuable to illustrate ways in which the drinking problem is not the "only problem" but how pervasive its effects are. This helps to set the stage for the need and value of incorporating everyone into the treatment process. Areas identified to illustrate the widespread pervasiveness of the problem are the children's grades; the children's behavior; relationships with in-laws and friends; accidents at home or work; financial problems; health problems; decrease in sexual desire and activity; and job performance.

A cautionary note needs to be communicated regarding involvement with the nonalcoholic spouse in this process. Her self-esteem and sense of value is probably significantly diminished by the time she initiates contact. Assuming the individual affording assistance possesses at least a mild degree of competence, she is likely to have found the therapeutic relationship very different and rewarding. Even though there may have been discomfort for her as she developed insight into the situation, she has been listened to and affirmed by the person affording assistance. The author believes it is only natural that the nonalcoholic spouse might develop a positive transference and perhaps not want to share this "new relationship" of hers. By "sharing" it with the alcoholic, this relationship may also be destroyed as so many others have been in the past. For this reason, it does not seem unrealistic to experience some mild resistance from the spouse about involvement of others in the therapeutic relationship/process. The clinician must deal with this transition point in a sensitive fashion so as not to have her perceive the "additions" as rejection of her. Certainly her perceiving herself as being rejected is not what she needs at this point, and it may also increase the likelihood of her sabotaging efforts to engage the rest of the family.

The remainder of this chapter will be designed to provide concerns regarding means of enlisting the family into the treatment process. While the preceding discussion focused on the nonalcoholic spouse as being the point of initial contact with the alcoholic and family, the following ideas are also applicable to those situations where some other family member, or the alcoholic, is the initial contact person.

Prior to engaging in this discussion, the author wants to emphasize the role of the counselor in the process of engaging total families. Oftentimes families are not involved in the treatment process and the lack of involvement is attributed to the family's "resistance." The author believes that this is caused more because of the counselor's uncertainty and anxiety than of any characteristics of the family. Counselors who have not adequately resolved their own family struggles are likely to be uneasy sitting with other families, and their uneasiness gets communicated in the process of attempting to recruit. As a result, it is as though these families are doing the counselor a "favor" by not coming and confronting him/her with the uneasiness and anxiety which family process stimulates in them. For this reason, counselors need to assess their own intrapersonal comfort level with families and also attempt to bolster their skills in working with families. Berg and Rosenblum (1977) determined in their study that the success with which therapists were able to recruit entire families was positively correlated with the degree of training the therapist had in marriage and family therapy. Certainly the results of this study should not be surprising in light of the fact that none of us seem too excited to engage in activities in which we perceive ourselves as being incompetent.

Recruiting Considerations

In recruiting families, the counselor must be resolute in both believing in the value of family involvement and his/her competence in dealing with them. It is the counselor who should decide who will attend sessions and not the family's contact person. Without the counselor making this determination, it is not unlikely to suspect that only certain coalitions and alliances will be in attendance. This issue relates to what Whitaker (1967) refers to as the "battle for structure," or determining the how and what of the therapeutic process. If counselors are not able to establish themselves as capable of exercising this prerogative at this point, it is not unreasonable to expect that they will be further neutered by the family. There is also research documenting that the more members present in the initial family session, the greater the likelihood of engaging the entire family in the treatment endeavor (Sager, 1968; Stanton and Todd, 1980).

While there are some who believe the contact person should be responsible for encouraging the rest of the family into treatment, the author believes the counselor must take an active and direct role in the recruitment process. In recruiting families with an alcoholic member, it seems especially crucial to actively involve one's self and initiate contacts personally. While the phone can be used for this purpose, there are many times when nothing short of a home visit will suffice for purposes of recruitment. As Stanton and Todd (1980) have indicated, this active role by the counselor eliminates the need for a family member attempting to explain the need/value of the total family involvement when they may not be certain of it themselves. It also provides the counselor an opportunity to dispel any uncertainties or concerns family members may have prior to their attendance at the first session. It is the author's experience that more than one contact may be necessary in involving these families and that persistence and an increased tolerance for frustration are valuable assets at this juncture of the treatment process. Stanton and Todd (1980), in their work with families of addicts, determined that there was an average of 6.7 contacts with the addict and other family members in attempting to engage the entire family. These contacts consisted of phone calls, home visits, and/or sessions with the addict or other family member for purposes of recruiting. The number of contacts in their work ranged from 1 to 33. While this effort may be regarded as difficult, it is probably safe to say that the effort is at least as time consuming as it is difficult, and thus the need for persistence.

Along with persistence and an ability to join the family, it should be obvious that there is also need for administrative support of the time necessary to engage in the recruitment effort. In most cases, the time utilized in these efforts would not be a "billable" effort, but certainly can be justified with regards to efficacy and effectiveness of treatment (see Chapter 1).

Davis (1977-78), Van Deusen, and others (1979) have documented how the sooner the family is contacted in relation to an intake, the greater the likelihood of total family involvement. It seems that not only is there a type of imprinting with regards to who the professional is that does the first contacting, but it is also likely that the family is involved in or close to a crisis, which probably results in them being more amenable to assistance. As their defenses are in a state of confusion, they may also be most open to outside assistance in realigning themselves into a more functional "whole."

In contacting the family, the counselor should be careful not to convey a sense of blame. More than likely they already experience guilt regarding their involvement, or lack of same, with the alcoholic and to intensify this is more likely to alienate than it is to engage the family. While this may run counter to how many in the alcohol field tend to operate, it seems from the author's experience to be an essential approach. The family should be informed of the value, if not necessity, of their involvement to assist the counselor. After all, they have known the alcoholic much longer and more intimately than the counselor. It is this knowledge of the client, their concern, and other assistance that is needed. To struggle with the family about their involvement in "the problem" at this point is almost assuredly going to be counterproductive. To approach them as "healthy" people, rather than "patients," can greatly facilitate the recruitment and treatment effort.

Along these lines, it can be valuable to convey to the family that the primary goal is that of "helping the alcoholic" and not that of "straightening out the family." In most cases the family has come to be organized around the "problem" of the alcoholic in their midst and it is for the reason of ameliorating this problem for which they are most likely to become involved in treatment. Haley (1976) has extensively discussed the value of identifying and accepting the primary concern/goal of the family as the most facilitative means of engaging and maintaining their commit-ment to treatment. After identifying what they are most interested in achieving (sobriety, family/marital stability, employment, free of legal entanglements, etc.), it is important to be able to convey to the family how total group involvement will facilitate and expedite this effort. At this point the counselor may feel as though a "sales" job is being conducted, and it is not unreasonable to define this stage of the recruitment process as being just that. Naturally the mere fact of the effort expended by the counselor in engaging the family can be a tremendous nonverbal way of conveying to the family that the counselor believes their "assis-tance" is important, if not vital, to the treatment effort.

From here, the author would like to direct his attention to concerns regarding the recruitment of specific family subsystems into the treatment effort. The author is indebted to the work of Stanton and Todd (1980) in providing this structure and some of the following ideas.

Recruiting Parents

In recruiting parents of, for instance, an adolescent abuser, special pains must be taken to not ally with the adolescent against the parents. As indicated earlier, the parents are probably already experiencing self-blame, and the slightest sensation of blame from a counselor could be sufficient to insure their not being engaged. The effort should be geared to joining them in an effort to assist their son and daughter to becoming "more responsible" or whatever other language they may tend to use. In enlisting the parents, it is not at all unreasonable for the counselor to talk of the tough job of parenting in this "day and age" with the omnipresence of drugs and the sanction drugs seem to have from "kids" today. The counselor who is a parent can perhaps utilize this shared experience with the parents as a means of joining them.

The parents may have been approached and/or involved in previous treatment that was geared at confronting and shaming them. For this reason, sensitivity is important along with a convincing approach regarding the "difference" of involvement in this treatment effort. It can be valuable to convey to the parents that they have the "right" to be involved in their child's treatment along with the realization that they have so much to contribute as a result of the length of time they have known their youngster. The author has found it valuable to convey to parents that he could work alone with the adolescent, but that he would "certainly be handcuffed" in the treatment effort without the aid of the knowledge they possess about the individual. Continuing, it is also of value to convey that "while I am concerned about your youngster's welfare, I know there is no way that I can be as concerned as you parents are." While this may not necessarily be the case, most parents sense that resisting involvement at this point would convey that they are not even as concerned for their youngster as is this "stranger."

Recruiting Fathers

Whenever possible, it is best to approach the parents together. The author realizes this may mean an evening contact, in light of father's daytime work schedules, but experience suggests the investment is worthwhile. So often mothers, when approached individually, will indicate father's lack of interest and/or availability. While the mother's motivation may be that of protecting the father, and/or enhancing her own status by her apparent availability, it has been the author's experience that dad's "unavailability" is just not true. When these "resistant, unavailable" fathers have been approached, more often than not they indicate their availability and interest; they had either not been informed by their wives, or else misinformed, i.e. "I was told my presence was not really important." The author's experience suggests that fathers tend to be more pragmatic and concrete in their orientations, and for this reason a "reality rub" seems to often be effective with them. (Reality rub is used here to indicate direct communication about the danger that their abusing son or daughter is in. The danger may be that of serious legal confrontation and/or death of their youngster unless direct and immediate attention is given the matter.)

Berg and Rosenblum's study (1977) has validated the value of engaging fathers in the treatment process. They determined that families attending an intake without the father dropped out of treatment significantly more often than those where father was also in attendance initially. Another significant difference occurred in the area of family involvement depending upon when father became involved. Fathers who attended the intake tended to stay in the treatment process significantly more often than those fathers who did not attend until some point after the first session. These findings convey to this author the value of extending the extra effort often required in order to recruit fathers into the treatment effort from the beginning.

Recruiting Mothers

More often than not, it will be the mother who seems most aware and involved in the adolescent's abuse. For this reason they seem easier to engage than fathers, and there also seems to be a social expectation of "mothers should be available to assist their youngsters," which operates to facilitate their involvement. The apparent overextension of the mother can often be used to join her. A statement such as: "It is obvious that you have done everything in your power and certainly suffered more than your share already" can comprise "just what the doctor ordered" to insure mother's commitment to this treatment effort and the counselor. By accentuating her concern and knowledge of the youngster of concern, she quickly comes to perceive the counselor as knowing what needs to be done and one that can be trusted.

Recruiting Children

Children are generally responsive to parents requests for assistance. This is especially true of a request from their nonalcoholic parent. While, occasionally, older children may be hesitant of being overly involved and/or being forced to take sides, they are also aware enough to listen to the counselor's explanation of what their involvement will consist. It is as important with the children as it is with parents to inform them of what the treatment effort will entail and to dispel whatever concerns and uncertainties they may have. Children, in particular, seem to be concerned with determining a sense of confidence in the counselor's strength and ability to contend with their family. It seems likely that their parents, as their most immediate adult models, have not demonstrated the strength and competence necessary to manage the family, so the children are now looking for some assurance of the counselor's ability to do so.

The process of recruiting families, while not necessarily pleasant, is not an insurmountable task. As mentioned previously, it is more time consuming than it is difficult or complex. When working with the alcoholic and family, the author believes that directive and active recruiting should be expected as more typical than atypical. Certainly this may cause a rethinking of many philosophical constructs of some who have practiced therapy, but the author believes the following quote emphasizes the need for this consideration.

> Denial is a living part of alcoholism and of the family. We cannot wait for the alcoholic to stop drinking before we initiate treatment for the family members; we cannot wait for the problem drinker to quit denying the problem before we initiate a program of help. A promise for treatment of a disease whose most prevailing symptom is denial in both the victim and the family members cannot wait for the motivation of the alcoholic (Howard and Howard, 1978, p. 143).

SUMMARY

This chapter was devoted to the development of an understanding of the family's adjustment to alcoholism and the various difficulties in enlisting total family involvement in treatment. The seven stages of a family's adjustment to alcoholism (Jackson, 1954) were discussed, with specific attention to the following in each stage: the alcoholic's status, the spouse's reaction and other behavior; impact upon the children; what treatment potential, if any, there appears to be. The second section of this chapter addressed concerns the author believes awareness of is important in order to enhance recruitment of the entire family. Specific attention was directed to concerns regarding recruitment of parents as a subsystem, fathers and mothers individually, and children.

Chapter 5

ADOLESCENTS AND CHEMICAL ABUSE

INTRODUCTION

Family therapy is essential with the drug-using adolescent. In
every instance where I have a youngster that abuses drugs, there is
a family problem from the simple, obvious factor of family drug
use, which a youngster can emulate and identify with, to the kind
of tensions, hypocrisy, unhappiness, lack of communication in
the home, which can also be conducive in pushing a youngster
into drugs as one way of coping or adjusting. Opening lines of
communication between parent and youngster is one extremely
important factor in the treatment of drug abuse (Gould in
Gamage, 1973, p. 53).

IN THE ABOVE statement Dr. Robert Gould has stated the
beliefs of this author regarding adolescent chemical abuse.
While being fully cognizant of adolescence as a time for the
individual to begin the move out of the family, when abuse is
involved in the process, this should serve as a warning signal that
there is a likely dysfunction in the family. If the adolescent is
unable to engage in the normally expected testing of limits and
boundaries in an effort to disengage the family without abuse
occurring, it is likely the family is functioning in a growth-
retarding fashion. While it may be inferred that it is only the
adolescent who is being retarded from achieving growth and
maturation, this is unlikely.

As Gould states, there is a high likelihood of family drug
misuse and/or the presence of "tensions, hypocrisy, unhappiness,
lack of communication in the home," which are contributing to
the adolescent's abuse. It seems myopic to believe that the

69

presence of any of these variables in a family unit would prove to be stifling to only one member. The very process of adapting to these stressers obviously requires the utilization of psychic energy and other resources that could otherwise be applied and available for more creative and functional endeavors by all. Adolescents are often the ones who do get identified though, as they are involved in the process of moving out from the family as their basic unit and into the community.

An old belief in the early child guidance movement was that "whenever there is a disturbed child, there is likely a disturbed marriage/family, although not all disturbed marriages/families produce disturbed children." The essence of this statement being that occasionally, and for whatever the reason, some children seem to be resilient enough to escape the web of a disturbed marriage/family without being disturbed themselves, but if you have a disturbed child you are likely to find a disturbed marriage/family within which that child resides. Based upon his experience, the author believes this axiom to be true with almost no exceptions. Consequently it follows that to treat the adolescent abuser without involving the family would be difficult at best (if not impossible) if it is expected the adolescent will either continue to live at home while involved in treatment or be returned home upon completion of treatment. Carl Whitaker said the following while discussing what, if any, contraindications there are for family therapy with an adolescent population:

> This author (Whitaker) is convinced that there are no contraindications if the family is available and if the therapist is willing to struggle with the whole unit. This is probably true whether the identified patient is an adolescent or an adult but is certainly most obvious in the treatment of the adolescent. The family is the controlling agent in any adolescent's life—far out of proportion to time spent with them, and in spite of physical distance (Whitaker, 1975, p. 207).

While those of us who treat abusers, or dependent individuals, might like to talk about individual responsibility, choice, free will, and other equally noble tenets of mankind, we must always keep in mind the power of the family unit as a shaper and determinant of our behavior. We might do a tremendous job of changing perceptions and other dimensions of a person's mental set while in treatment, only to find "all that work" quicklv undone once the person returns to their old home environment where no changes have occurred that should foster what we perceive as a more healthy way of being and behaving for that person. Indeed, in a general way, the changes we facilitated while the person was involved in treatment may have been deemed valuable by all outsiders, but to the family the changes just do not "fit" with how they operate. The adolescent who returns from treatment talking and behaving in a responsible, more independent fashion deprives mother of the one source of gratification she had in life. Now that the adolescent is more responsible and independent, mother is confronted with the "emptiness" she feels and begins to behave in a way that makes it difficult for dad to escape into work or other activities as easily as he could do in the past. The homeostasis (or equilibrium) of the family's balance is upset and mechanisms are set into motion that are designed to have the adolescent resume the old "dysfunctional" behaviors, including using drugs again.

As this past example portrays the occurrence of treatment effect being reversed when an adolescent was the object of treatment efforts, the following serves to illustrate adolescent abuse secondary to a slightly different "wrinkle." An adolescent was referred to the author for treatment revolving about an abusive pattern of drug usage that had been identified by a school counselor. The adolescent was a sixteen-year-old male who had been a good strong student and was functioning well in all facets of school until about three months prior to the referral. In the first session my concern was with determining the nature and degree of use, as well as the presence of confounding circumstances. In determining the presence of drug abuse, as opposed to use or experimentation, the primary concern is if the drug intake interferes with a person's normal way of life and the adolescent's growth and development. As Gould has stated: "When he's having difficulty with his peer relations, when he's having difficulty in school because of drugs, when he is having difficulty doing everyday activities which are gratifying and lead to growth and development, then he is taking drugs to a point where he is abusing himself" (Gamage, 1973, p. 43). It was quickly determined that this sixteen-year-old's life was suffering in all facets as a result of use and preoccupation with drug ingestion. Upon inquiring about confounding or precipitating circumstances it was learned that his father had gone into inpatient treatment for alcoholism about one year earlier. The father's treatment had resulted in his sobriety and a reportedly much improved marriage. While this had occurred for the father, there had been some interesting shifts required. The primary shift, with direct relevance for this sixteen-year-old, was that prior to the father's treatment, the son—he was the eldest of four siblings—was the surrogate father; mother was very reliant upon him for both physical assistance around the house and emotional nurturance. Once father returned home and assumed the responsibilities, Dale (the sixteen-year-old) felt rejected and as though he no longer had a useful or functional role to fill in the family. As a result of Dale being parentified (or pulled into an adult role early in his life), he had never really learned how to relate to his peers in age appropriate ways when he was under stress. Once he felt without a "place," drugs seemed to be a way of effectively numbing his sense of gnawing emptiness and hurt and happened to be easily accessible to him in school. The "drug culture" in his school was quick to receive him because of the money he had and the ease with which he shared his money with them in order to gain the acceptance he felt he had lost in his family. Also the author could not help but wonder if Dale had turned to drugs as a result of observing and modeling the way in which his father had adapted to stress by abusing alcohol.

As a result of this session with Dale, family therapy was initiated. Fourteen sessions, spread over a four-month period, resulted in Dale being drug free; he returned to his functional behavior in the school setting. The entire family, including Dale, reported they felt much more positive and optimistic about their family. It is now two years later and Dale is still drug free, with the exception of an occasional beer with his college freshman friends. Dale's father had been involved in a treatment program that identified itself as "family oriented," but never involved Dale and his siblings in any sessions after the initial intake. The remainder of the treatment focused on Dale's father and included the mother.

While Dale is one case, the author has been involved in other similar cases and had numerous others reported to him where treatment of the parent alcoholic has been successful in achieving sobriety but has also been closely followed by an adolescent family member beginning to abuse drugs. The author believes these cases are a loud voice in support of the essential nature of involving the family in treatment. While it is difficult to say with empirical certainty, it seems very plausible to assume that had Dale's family not been involved in the treatment process, one or more of Dale's siblings may have also become involved in abusing drugs and/or father's sobriety becoming significantly threatened, if not blatantly broken. Dale's drug use had also reached a point of being abusive. It seems certain that without intervention, addiction would have evolved in this case.

· The New Directions program in Santa Barbara, California has identified the need and value of involving the families of adolescent abusers in the treatment process (NIAAA/IFS, Dec. 31, 1979, p. 5). Wayne Muller, the program's director, states that the family is considered the best target for both primary and secondary prevention. Not only is the abuser reached, but siblings are identified as being at risk, too. This program has documented itself as successful in the form of an 87 percent reduction in the number of alcohol-related arrests among the youngsters identified as problem drinkers.

The case of Dale also illustrates the importance of early identification and referral of a suspected abusing adolescent. Erikson (1950) has spoken of the negative group identity and its prominence, particularly in adolescence. Without early identification and intervention, there is significant concern for adolescents coming to perceive themselves as "dopers," "heads," or other similar connotations. It is as though the adolescent's basic identity comes to be associated with drugs and the ritualistic behavior that accompanies drug use. If the adolescent's identity has crystallized about drugs and their use over a longer period of time, it has been the author's experience that the course of treatment is likely going to be longer, with a need to bring to therapeutic application other tools such as inpatient treatment with therapeutic application of community and group involvement, in conjunction with the family therapy.

While this chapter was being written, the December, 1979 and January, 1980 issue of *The Voice*—a Wisconsin association on alcohol and other drug abuse newsletter—was received by the author. The two lead, front-page stories dealt with the report of various studies on the impact of parents and families on teenage drinking problems. The numerous studies cited emphasized the family as being the single most prominent influence in adolescent drinking and abuse. Certainly the role of the peer group in the adolescent's life and the past and present influence of the adolescent's family will shape and determine how the peer group is perceived and responded to by each teenager. As an example, if the adolescent has not developed a strong sense of identity through experiencing both a sense of belongingness and sep-arateness in the family, it is unreasonable to expect the teenager to be able to say "no" appropriately. If the adolescent does not have a strong sense of self and familial support and understanding, drug abuse is certainly more likely to occur.

Along with the above-identified belief, there is cause for concern regarding the adolescent taking unresolved issues from the family of origin and replaying them in the family they develop in adulthood, as well as in other relationships they experience. Whitaker has said the following about the adolescent who leaves the family without achieving a productive resolution to the tensions present in the family:

> If an adolescent leaves his family in a self-induced puberty ceremony of rebellion, if he breaks with the family without some group resolution of the problems of the symbiosis amongst them, if he leaves without joining in an overt family effort to resolve his desertion—rather than by a therapeutic effort to relieve the individual and group stress—he is stuck with guilt and not free to instigate a new and creative life. He may then be compelled to reconstruct the old family again, to work out that senior year and that graduation ceremony at work, at play or in his marriage (Whitaker, 1975, p. 201).

INTERVENTION

The two primary family types that adolescent abusers come from are the fused (or enmeshed) type and the disengaged (or fragmented) type. In the fused family it often seems true that adolescents turn to drugs as a means of numbing the sense of suffocation and stultification they experience. The changes that accompany adolescence prove threatening to the family's overly rigid sense of security and togetherness. Reacting to this threat they tighten the hold on the adolescent, which stimulates the teenager into looking for "relief." Helm Stierlin (1974) has referred to this "tightening" process as activation of centripetal forces by the family. The family attempts to pull and tie the youngster into the core of the family just at the time when the developmental task for the youngster is that of moving out. This conflict is what the youngster turns to drugs for relief from. The disengaged family results in adolescents who sense a prominent emptiness and lack of belongingness. Stierlin refers to this family type as operationalizing centrifugal forces that spin or throw out the members. The emptiness and hurt of these adolescents can be numbed by the effect of the drugs, and the drug culture adolescents involve themselves in may provide them with the first real sense of belongingness they have experienced. Adolescent abusers are also seen who seem to have become involved with drugs, but do not come from families who seem to be either fused or disengaged. It has been the author's experience that many times these adolescents are responding to significant environmental stresses that need to be managed more appropriately. An example of this latter type is Lisa, a fourteen-year-old. After the initial referral and contact with the entire family it was learned that one month prior to her beginning to abuse drugs her father had lost his job and her mother's mother (who was significant to the whole family) had died. Lisa started using drugs upon breaking up with her boyfriend of one year, just prior to a major school function which was boy-girl in nature. It seemed that numerous environmental circumstances had befell this family and Lisa at an inordinate rate. All evidence suggested that Lisa's loss of her boyfriend would have been handled, with the family's support, by her in the past. Unfortunately, at a time when she was most in need of her parents, her parents were preoccupied with other major adjustments in their own lives and not as available as they otherwise would have been.

While there are these three prominent family types out of which adolescent abuse seems to emanate (enmeshed/fused, disengaged/fragmented, and situationally stressed), there are basic considerations for effective therapeutic intervention that are relevant to all.

Those who have worked in the area of alcoholism treatment for any period of time are familiar with the term *bringing up the bottom*, i.e., the most effective intervention is often that which "makes things worse" or intensifies the discomfort; until the discomfort is increased, there is no motivation for change, perceived or felt. In the treatment of adolescents, placement—separating the family and adolescent—can frequently be a means of "bringing up the bottom" for all concerned. The placement may be an adolescent crisis intervention center, alcoholism or other drug abuse treatment center, temporary foster placement, or some other similar setting. The author has observed on many occasions how this short-term placement has opened the eyes of the entire family to the "seriousness and need for change" before something more significant occurs. It is at this time (the time of crisis) that the family is most shaken and susceptible to both perceiving the need for change and beginning to act upon it, and we in helping positions must be prepared to capitalize on. So often reports are heard of adolescents being placed in some setting and being effectively limited from contact with the family or vice versa. It is at this time that there is the greatest potential for the family to come together in a different way for the first time. While this is a time rich in creative potential for change, it is also a time that can prove taxing to the helper involved.

The author can recall an incident where he was involved with a sixteen-year-old male named Bob who was placed in a primarily adult psychiatric unit because of lack of a more appropriate facility for adolescents. He had been drinking heavily and was picked up by the police while he was in a disoriented, extremely drunken state on the streets and in need of medical attention. Upon receiving medical attention, and involved in the detoxification process, his parents were brought in. After soliciting assurance of his physical well-being they began to unleash a verbal tirade about his irresponsibility, rebelliousness, and other similar blasts and numerous unanswered questions. It was determined that Bob had experienced numerous other drunken episodes in the last six months. While acknowledging their position as parents, and their justified anger, the author wanted to communicate his ability to control what was turning into a chaotic onslaught that would probably make Bob even more sullen and withdrawn than he already was. For this reason the parents were asked to leave the room temporarily. While I wanted to talk with Bob alone, to place his parents anger in the perspective of their being concerned, I also wanted to communicate to both Bob and his parents that I was capable of handling the situation. If the helper, in this type of situation, appears to be overwhelmed, it is unlikely that the family will entrust themselves to the professional, and understandably so. Specifically I wanted to demonstrate to Bob that I was capable of defending him by directing his parents out of the immediate, emotionally laden field. At this point I was intentionally and physically involving myself in what Zuk (1971) refers to as the "go-between process." Zuk says of the go-between process, ". . . conflict is a characteristic and inevitable phase of group life and that it is in the interest of the principals to take steps, secretively or publicly, to check its magnitude. One of the steps is the search for and selection of a party empowered to mediate" (1971, p. 45). He also states that power is a primary variable here and that he suggests a working definition is ". . . the capacity to initiate actions leading to a predicted increase in control. The concept of therapeutic power will mean the capacity of the therapist to define the therapist-patient relationship in ways he believes to be in the best interest of the patient" (Zuk, 1971, p. 45). Without my exercising power or control to change the interaction that was occurring, I was comfortable in assuming that what would develop would be "more of the same." The mother continuing with her verbal barrage, Bob withdrawing and becoming more sullen, mother intensifying her verbage, Bob withdrawing more, and on and on. As this would be frustrating and counterproductive, my concern is also that they will (not necessarily consciously) come to perceive an inability in me to help them be different in any way from how they usually are. As Andolfi has stated: ". . . when the family starts therapy, it requires 'emotional guarantees' before it becomes accessible and permits entrance to the therapist. The therapist, therefore, must acquire contractual power and credibility if he is to be accepted by the family members as an agent of change" (1979, p. 147). At this time it was as blatantly obvious to me, as it was to them, that what they had been doing had not been successful.

After separating them and determining from Bob that what I had just observed was typical, I emphasized the problem by stating it was getting them all no where fast and him almost dead. I then met with the parents and initially joined them by acknowledging their anger as being justified, but elaborated upon what I guessed were other emotions they were experiencing such as hurt, fear, and embarrassment. It has been my frequent experience that families of adolescent abusers are overwhelmed with anger and never acknowledge or communicate the other emotions that are also simultaneously present. It is necessary to join the parents initially to engage them into the therapeutic process. To just confront at this point would be counterproductive and likely drive them out of potential treatment. The joining serves as the anesthetic or shock absorber to the treatment effort and better insures that therapeutic interventions will take as a result of a reduced level of defenses on their part. From here, as with Bob, the urgency and seriousness of the matter was accentuated with them and followed by the suggestion that Bob be allowed to stay a few days for observation. At this time they were invited for a session the next morning. After they agreed they were reunited with their son where I made two requests—both of which I perceive as important to this type of treatment. I informed them of my need for them to bring in the two younger children in the family. I then told them (as I typically will) that it was important for me to see everyone so that I can get a more complete and total perspective and understanding and also that I was sure they were and had been effected by similar situations in the past. I also gave them an assignment (other than just bringing the rest of the family), and this assignment was directed to Bob as well as the family. They were all asked to recall what, specifically, they (each individually) had attempted to do in order to change this type of behavior in the past. I gave them this assignment so that indeed I would discover what they had attempted to do in the past, but also to begin to counter what appeared to be a pattern with them (a not uncommon one)—that being a prominent tendency to have an external, projecting orientation and blaming others rather than examining one's own role in a situation. I was countering this by asking them to become introspective and look at only themselves. This assignment would also give me clues as to how involved each person is in the family (at least with regards to this situation) by what they were able to provide as changes they have attempted to make.

The family did return the next morning and a two-and-one-half hour session was engaged in. While I continued to emphasize the urgency and seriousness of the circumstances, I also was sensitive to communicating and accentuating what I perceived as hopeful signs, i.e. they all did return; they each had given thought to the assignment; and, as tough as things had been in their family over the last six months, they continued to hang together; and they had overcome other serious ordeals. In the process of talking with them, I asked them if they (the parents) had ever been in similarly tough situations. They indicated that the first two years of their marriage had been rough due to serious interference by the husband's alcoholic father. I like to determine other "tough times" in order to underscore and remind them that they have "made it" before. Too often it is easy, in the midst of turmoil, for families to forget that they have "made it" before and there is significant value in reminding them of this at stressful times. It is also surprising how often they can recall specific methods of resolution once utilized, but since forgotten.

During the initial stage of this session, behavior was manifested which is frequently observed in families with an adolescent abuser. The mother was questioning Bob and demanding answers, which he predictably withheld. A manifestation of the "insist-resist" cycle so often witnessed between parent and teenager. The more the parent insists, the more the adolescent resists, and so on. This pattern was short-circuited by intercepting and saying to Bob that I did not want him to answer, but rather guessed the mother knew the answers and asked her to provide them. I do this for two reasons: (1) to make for more legitimate interaction. I assume the mother does know the answers but is attempting to "show me," which humiliates the adolescent and diminishes the likelihood of him becoming involved spontaneously; (2) I also do this to protect the adolescent's integrity and communicate to him that I can control the flow of interaction in the family. I believe, as already mentioned, that with his increased perception of me as a potential powerful ally, the likelihood of his spontaneous involvement, and sense of hope, are simultaneously enhanced.

The outcome of the session consisted of identifying Bob as having an abusive pattern of drinking and one in need of change; a plan of action consisting of his involvement with AA and a group for adolescents with drug abuse problems and for the entire family to continue in family therapy. While both mother and father were only very occasional users of drugs, and that primarily a social glass of wine, Bob's grandfather was a chronic alcoholic. From involvement with this family it became apparent that on Bob's father's side of the family there was a chronic male alcoholic every other generation as far back as he could trace. As Bowen (1974), and others have identified, it is amazing how often similar patterns reoccur in families and are likely to continue to do so unless intercepted by some means.

The treatment of Bob's family did result in his terminating the abuse of alcohol and ended by rather intense, concentrated therapy with his mother and father. It seemed that since their first two years of struggling with the husband's alcoholic father (who eventually died) they had lost contact with one another and drifted apart with father involved in his work and mother raising the children. The treatment of the adolescent abuser's family terminating with marital therapy is an often observed phenomena, as the focus shifts from the immediate crisis or concern over the abuse, to the whole family involvement, to the architects of the family—the parents.

As with the case with Bob, AA and group therapy are powerful treatment allies to family therapy. As mentioned in Chapter 3, it has been this author's experience that used in conjunction with one another a powerful synergistic effect is stimulated with results greater than what any of the approaches individually applied could engender.

Berenson (1976) has discussed two types of adolescent drinking. The first type is characterized by the adolescent who is abusing but resides in a family with no significant past or present history of alcoholism. The second type of adolescent drinking is distinguished from the first on the basis of drinking problems being present in the parental subsystem as well. The author concurs with Berenson in his belief that the second type is more difficult to treat and the one in which AA, group therapy, and perhaps inpatient treatment will all need to be applied with family therapy in order to be successful. In the first type identified by Berenson, family therapy as described in this book is usually successful. One element of successful treatment with this type of adolescent drinker is reciprocal social contracting such as that described by Stuart (1971). In this approach the members of the family, and in particular the drinking adolescent and the parents, are involved in developing contracts involving exchanges of behaviors and positively perceived rewards for the achievement of specified changes.

As far as determining degree of severity of the problem, a tool devised by Mayer and Filstead (1979) appears to hold some promise. The Adolescent Alcohol Involvement Scale (AAIS) while only consisting of fourteen questions with a multiple choice response option, has demonstrated itself to be a reliable tool in discriminating among adolescents who manifest various intensities of involvement with alcohol. While need for further study is evident, the AAIS seems to offer much potential for those concerned with differentiating degrees of involvement with alcohol by adolescents. Naturally the data yielded from administration of this tool could be of assistance in determining the type of treatment that may most effectively be utilized with the adolescent also.

At times the author has been asked about treatment of the adolescent who is abusing and comes from a single parent family. A 1979 study released by the National Council on Alcoholism clearly documented that adolescents from broken homes show more prevalence of drinking, more frequent drinking, and more problem drinking than teenagers whose parents are still together. This should not be too surprising when we consider that along with the single parent family goes a greater incidence of variables such as economic impoverishment and the resulting frustrations, less parental time available for attending to children, and, a deficiency, in most cases, of both sex models. While these characteristics are also true of many intact families, the incidence is more prominent in the single parent family. In light of these past observations, it is important to realize that the principles and constructs previously identified in this writing are as applicable to the single parent family as they are to the intact family. With the single parent family, outside groups such as Parents Without Partners or AA can be particularly valuable in helping the single parent begin to give the adolescent room to disengage from the family in an age appropriate fashion. So often the single parent becomes overly invested in the adolescent to the detriment of the adolescent appropriately individuating. This type of situation could be characterized as enmeshed or fused when considering the boundaries between adolescent and parent. The "over investment" makes it difficult, at best, for the adolescent to engage in age appropriate activities. Just as this is often the case with the single parent family, the converse, or lack of investment, is also frequently observed. As the single parent attempts to organize and conduct the business necessary to maintain a family, they become overwhelmed and unable to be available to their children in the way both they and their children would like. In this case we are talking of a disengaged family with regards to the boundaries between parent and children. With this situation, the services provided by county social service agencies such as homemaker assistance, financial management, and direct economic assistance can be particularly valuable. Through the application of this type of assistance the single parent is able to move beyond feeling quite so overwhelmed and become more available to the children.

STAGES OF TREATMENT

In applying a family therapy approach to the treatment of adolescents with drug problems there seem to be rather predictable stages in the therapeutic process. While this is presented in the context of treating adolescents, these same principles are observed in family therapy regardless of the age of the index patient. These stages, while implying a linear type connection, must be regarded as guideposts and certainly not as "cast in stone." Working with families is a dynamic and fluid process so overlap and exceptions to these stages should be expected. The eight elements to be presented now are closely analogous to those presented by McPherson, Brackelmanns, and Newman (1974) and the author is grateful to them for their original contribution.

Setting the Stage for Family Treatment

Most frequently the initial involvement with the adolescent will come about as a result of direct concern for alcohol-drug misuse or related behaviors. There are those infrequent occasions when the author receives a referral where the family, or at least most, present themselves as having significant family disturbance in need of change as well as the adolescents' alcohol-drug problem. When this is not the case the therapist needs to be sensitive in how the entire family is involved. The author will frequently ask the entire family in for the initial interview under the auspices of: "This is necessary for me to get as much information and as complete an understanding as possible in order that something can be done as quickly as possible. Without everyone being present I am significantly handicapped." Regardless of what you may already know about the situation, it is important to initially accept the family's (or family spokesperson's) definition of "what's the matter." As the stage for family involvement is set it is to be expected that many "reasons" for members not being able to make it to the session will be offered and these reasons must be met firmly. Reasons such as conflicting work schedules, "oh, he's not interested," "they're too young," and other such offerings, can most frequently be resolved by the therapist being firmly resolute and basing the need for their attendance out of concern not only for the adolescent, but also by stating: "I am sure this has created headaches, concern, and sleepless nights for all of you, and I think it's only fair that you all get your chance to speak your peace and identify what you would like changed." While this does not create a sense of blame, nor is it likely to trigger their guilt, it does communicate concern and acknowledgment of their all being involved if in no other way than as a recipient of the "fall out."

Putting Treatment Into Gear

Once the family is together in the first session it is important to not "betray" them by placing blame or inducing guilt. There is a need for the therapist to establish oneself as being concerned, understanding, and strong enough to really be of assistance to them.

By asking each their perception of the problem and what is in need of change, an important beginning is established and the therapist can begin to observe how the family operates. It is at this time that observations such as the following can be made: What silencing mechanisms are used and by whom; What is the affective tone of the family; Who seems to be aligned with whom; Are they realistic in both their perception of the "problem" and means of solving it; What is it that is attributed to various family members ("He's the silent one. She's always a brat! They keep secrets."); and, Do they perceive themselves as perhaps being able to benefit from treatment, or is it just a "fix the patient" attitude?

In the case of the last question raised it is important to communicate, in a sensitive fashion, how the various members other than the adolescent seem to be hurting, angry, upset, etc., to such a degree that it seems important for all to continue to help each other. During this phase it is also generally quite easy to do what Stierlin has identified: "By pointing out again and again how the parents and their adolescent offspring fail to share such a common focus (similar perceptions), how they avoid listening to each other, and how they cannot confirm either agreement or disagreement, the therapist establishes himself as a facilitator of communication instead of the stern, guilt inducing and partial judge he is often expected to be. He becomes the chief reconciling agent" (Stierlin, 1977, p. 293). Through this process a rationale for their all continuing is established, and the therapist is established as a person who is indeed concerned for all of them and also capable of helping them to perceive and behave differently with one another.

Gaining Admission to the Family

There is often considerable overlap between the last element and this one. As the gears are set into motion the various behaviors made by the therapist may also be successfully, or otherwise, acquiring admission into the family. As admission is granted, the therapist begins to feel confident in taking more risks as far as behaviors such as confrontations, interpretations, and general style of presentation are concerned. It begins to "feel" as though there is a working alliance between therapist and family. The therapist can freely engage in side taking with assurance that the other family members are not overly threatened by this behavior and realize the therapist moves "about" the family with each member while appearing to not be overly allied with any one member of the subsystem to the detriment of another.

This element of the process will probably be somewhat erratic and punctuated by rejections by one individual, or subsystem, or another at various times. At one moment the therapist may be strongly accepted by the father and adolescent son, mildly accepted by mother and second oldest child, and rejected by the youngest. As the therapy moves on, these perceptions and feelings shift among the various members in accordance with what and how the therapist is facilitating the treatment.

Old Fences/Boundaries Are Broken and New Ones Constructed

As the treatment proceeds, a rather predictable phase is that of boundaries being changed. It is not uncommon to perceive the adolescent feeling more as though he/she "belongs" in the family—the interactions, perceptions, styles of interacting with one another, and the family affect change and become more positive. It is as though one or more members who have sensed themselves being isolated from others is now moving back in. Fathers are also frequently on the "outside" of the family, and it has been the author's experience, and resultant belief, that many adolescents have taken to alcohol misuse as a means of stirring things up enough to bring dad back into the family. Naturally, as described in Chapter 2, it is usually not just a process of dad/adolescent deciding to re-enter, but also included is the need for others to change in such a way that room is made for their admittance. An example of this being the father who is making advance to moving back into the family, but the mother not relinquishing any responsibility to provide him "room."

Sorting Out Roles

As the boundaries are readjusted, and more healthy interactions promoted, there is value and need to examine how each contributed to the "mess" that was evident before and how they might best insure that a similar happening can be avoided in the future. With the family where there is an adolescent with a drug problem, blame and projection are frequently observed, as illustrated in an earlier case presentation in this chapter. The strong external orientation serves to prevent each from looking at themselves and their own contribution to the development and maintenance of the counterproductive processes. As change occurs it is valuable to ask the family members to identify their own role/contribution in the current situation(s) and changes they believe they might make. As each person speaks for themselves, others are invited to share their perceptions. Also, as each person identifies what and how they would like to change to make for a more productive family, it is valuable to ask them for ways in which they believe others in the family may be of assistance to them in achieving their desired changes. While this serves to highlight individual responsibility, it also affords an opportunity to emphasize the potential resources each can be to the other.

The Children and Parents Become Clearly Identified

As mentioned earlier in this chapter, a frequent observance is that of the adolescent in the role of being overly involved with one or the other of the parents (most frequently mother). It is as though the adolescent is acting out the frustrations, anger, hurt, and depression that resides between the parents but goes unexpressed and unresolved. The case of Bob, discussed earlier in this chapter, is a fine example of this occurrence. As treatment proceeds, the adolescent can return to the child subsystem and become more involved in age appropriate tasks, and mother and father can go on with the enhancement of both their marital and parental relationship. This too is a sensitive operation as it is not unusual to find that the adolescent's identity is strongly invested in the role of "doper," "marital savior," or other equally negative self-attribution and is only reluctantly relinquished. Also, mother and father may be somewhat frightened by the potential for greater closeness and intimacy between them after years of no practice and collected hurts and frustrations.

Individuation of the Members

As the various members develop a new sense of closeness they also acquire a capacity for separateness and autonomy, which may prove disconcerting. As the adolescent moves out to become involved in age appropriate developmental tasks, this may prove frightening and stimulate old fears of resumed drinking or other abuse and which needs to be confronted. At this phase, confrontations regarding family members assumptions indicating they "know" the others motivations, intentions, feelings, and the means utilized to invalidate one another in this fashion are common therapeutic issues. The family needs to learn that individuation is a necessary developmental task for all members and one to be treasured and not interpreted as a hazard or betrayal to the unit.

The Family Moves On

The family and therapist come to a point where termination is agreed to and acted upon. The family needs to be rewarded for the effort and accomplishments they have provided one another. This seems appropriate for a couple of reasons: (1) assuming change has occurred, it did so because of their energy and willingness and should be so acknowledged; and (2) this also underlines the idea that change came about as a result of their efforts so that should they enter therapy again at a later time, they realize it will again require their effort and not simply "coming to be fixed" by someone else. At the time of termination, along with the celebration of their accomplishments, the author believes it is valuble to encourage them to think of ways and means that they might continue to enhance themselves beyond this treatment-venture.

The author believes it is appropriate to share perceptions on what they might continue to work on and how they might do whatever it is that is suggested. For some time it has seemed senseless, to this writer, for the therapist to have these perceptions and ideas but not share them with the family. Especially at the time of termination, the issue of concern over fostering dependency should no longer be an issue or rationale for not sharing information.

SUMMARY

This chapter was designed to focus on the place and value of family therapy with adolescents who are involved with drug use/misuse. The preventive nature of family therapy was presented along with frequently observed types of families from which adolescent abusers emanate. Attention was directed to the difference between adolescent abusers and users and the value of early identification.

Intervention issues and ideas were presented and accompanied by case illustrations. Among the issues presented, the following were examples: engaging the family into treatment; joining them initially and not going too fast while effectively "bringing up the bottom" as is necessary; controlling the chaotic family; beginning to change their communication patterns; and, the role of giving assignments while doing family therapy.

After a discussion of types of adolescent drinking and the treatment implications, attention was directed to rather predictable phases of treatment with the adolescent's family. Case specific examples were utilized to illustrate the phases of treatment presented.

Chapter 6

EVALUATION OF THE FAMILY WITH AN ALCOHOLIC

INTRODUCTION

T HE READER, at this point, should have perceived the importance attached to including the family when working with an alcoholic. The author believes this is particularly true in the area of evaluation. Before interventions can be implemented it is particularly important for the therapist to have a sense of the particular intervention ramifications. Questions such as the following must be addressed not only to enhance effectiveness, but also to insure more responsible helping by the helper. What are the apparent adaptive consequences of drinking in this family? (What are secondary gains, such as: mother and oldest son maintaining a symbiotic tie; dad and mother effectively maintaining emotional distance; mother being protected from being confronted with her lack of sexual responsiveness; and dad being allowed to remain as a child, both emotionally and operationally?) What are the rules governing change in this family? What are the various roles assigned in this family and how rigid are they? What are the most effective means and/or avenues for engaging this family? What alliances and/or coalitions are existent and are most available for change? What resources does the family appear to have available to them and how effectively do they utilize them?

David Reiss (1980) has hypothesized that perhaps 10 percent of families involved in family therapy deteriorate as a result of the experience. This author believes that whatever the number of families that deteriorate may be, it is likely that inadequate evaluation or diagnosis occurred prior to treatment. It is probable that the therapist "went into" the family with either a very limited understanding, or none at all, and the randomly attempted interventions upset the family in a counterproductive way.

EVALUATION TECHNIQUES

Considering this, a number of clinicians and researchers have identified ways of evaluating various components of family functioning. Minuchin and his colleagues (1967) have devised a number of task situations. Families are asked to collectively plan a menu or arrive at some agreement regarding how to spend a set amount of money. Watzlawick (1966) also creates situations to promote interaction so that the therapist might evaluate the family's processes and patterns of interaction. He believes strongly that the observed processes are more crucial than the content and that these same processes are demonstrated by the family as they complete the various assignments. Some of his tasks are asking the family to plan something they can all do together or asking the parents to teach the children the meaning of a particular proverb. Papp (1967) and Simon (1972) have each discussed the means by which family sculpting can be utilized for purposes of evaluation. Feelings, utilization of space, coalitions, and attitude are among the various dimensions of family life that can be evaluated with sculpting.

Various art therapy techniques have also been effectively employed in the process of evaluating families. Kwiatkowska (1967) has described the "joint family scribble" in which each family member does a quick scribble, followed by the entire family producing a collaborative effort. Rubin and Magnussen (1974) and Bing (1970) have also described the use of joint family drawings as a means of learning about families. Along these lines Irwin and Mallory (1979) have identified the "family puppet interview" as a valuable tool in assessing a family. A variety of puppets are made available to the family from which each is asked to select the ones of most interest to them. Once the selections are made they are asked to develop a story, which they will enact. Upon completion of the presentations the family is engaged in the process of discussing their own observations and associations to the experience with particular reference to how their story is reflective of them as a group. This technique has been found to be particularly valuable in observing the families decision-making procedures, symbolic communication, and other similar variables.

EVALUATION CHOICE POINTS

While tasks such as those discussed above are valuable, the reader must remember that the selection of various tasks assigned within the context of the evaluation is only one element in need of consideration. Reiss (1980) has identified various "choice points," or decisions, the clinician must make as consideration is given to the evaluation process. Naturally the clinician's manner of conceptualizing will determine the choice eventually made, but Reiss has offered his "choice points" in terms of polarities to illustrate the contrast between various theoretical orientations available: developmental vs. cross sectional; family direction vs. environment direction; crisis vs. character; pathology vs. competence; and thematic vs. behavioral.

The developmental vs. cross sectional choice point revolves about focussing on the family as it currently is or to attempt to develop a longitudinal view of its development. There seems to be a tendency today for clinicians to select the cross sectional and concentrating on how the family is today. The primary assumption of the cross sectional, or "now" focus, is that family patterns are enduring variables in families. While the "developmentalists" are very sensitive to developmental stages of families (see Solomon, 1973), those with the cross-sectional orientation also give acknowledgment to the stage in which the family is, but believe the patterns are of more importance.

Family direction vs. environment direction is concerned with the perspective of the family shaping its interactions with the surrounding community versus the surrounding community shaping the internal family interactions. This author believes this may be a moot issue when viewed from a general systems orientation giving regard to the mutual and reciprocal interaction of families and the surrounding community. While any particular clinician may give somewhat more weight to one or the other, it seems the reciprocity between community and family must be acknowledged. To focus on the internal family functioning and ignore the community, or vice versa, seems shortsighted at best. In doing an evaluation it seems imperative to give attention to not only the internal family dynamics and how these are operationalized in responding to or effecting the community or environmental constraints, but also in what way the community may be reciprocally, or independently, functioning to impact and/or respond to the family. The most productive understanding upon which treatment can be based probably comes from comprehending the interactive nature of the two.

The crisis vs. character choice point revolves about the concern of the more immediate difficulty or complaint (crisis) versus the enduring patterns of self-protection and adaptation (character). This author believes that in working with the family where alcoholism is prominent, it is valuable to initially assume a crisis orientation in order to communicate a sense of being problem-focused as opposed to being more diffuse. As the work is initiated, a more character-oriented stance can be adapted in order to attempt to insure more long lasting and developmental accomplishments. The experience of this author has been that those who operationalize a more character-oriented evaluation may frustrate the family and alcoholic with all the "talk and history taking" as opposed to moving toward action and change. Usually these families are frustrated and tired by the time they engage help and their expectation is that help will be quickly forthcoming.

Most family evaluations focus on "what is wrong" with the family whether the person's orientation is "character" in nature, or "crisis." The person with the "character orientation" is focusing on chronically present disruptive patterns, while the person with the "crisis orientation" is focussed on acute problems. From this, the reader can see that historically the pathology vs. competence choice point has been predominated by the pathology orientation. Looking for "what is wrong" has been prominent since Freud's early efforts at "uncovering" and then remediating. Recently, the efforts of Lewis and his colleagues (1976) have developed a rather clinically sophisticated, but easily understood, means of evaluating family competence. They have discriminated variables that seem to account for healthy family systems and have presented them in a reliable scaling format that makes for a handy cognitive map to be employed by the clinician. With this, and other similar aids available, it seems that more clinicians are beginning to focus on the assets of a family as well as the liabilities or weaknesses that may be present. Naturally once the strengths have been identified, the adroit clinician can work through the strengths in order to remediate the weaknesses.

Thematic vs. behavioral, as a checkpoint, is concerned with the dichotomy between observable human behavior as the point of concentration (behavioral) versus the perception of observable behavior as simply comprising surface phenomenon with what resides below the surface only being available to both the client and clinician after considerable effort is expended (thematic). The behavioral perspective emphasizes observable behaviors and expends efforts in identifying what are behaviors that promote distress and dissatisfaction and what are behaviors that promote positive feelings and a sense of good will. After this determination is made, efforts are expended to diminish the frequency of negative behaviors and to increase the frequency of occurrence of positive behaviors. The clinician working from the thematic perspective is more concerned with exploring and understanding the family's myths, underlying motivations, unresolved conflicts of the adults in this family with their parents, and other such dimensions that may be influencing and shaping the family's present behavior. Once this determination is arrived at, the interventions to effect change follow.

While the preceding identify various theoretical "choice points," it is also necessary to keep in mind other more mechanical, but no less important, considerations such as: (1) time allowed for the evaluation—Is the evaluation to be conducted in one session or over a prolonged period of time?; (2) context where the evaluation is conducted—Is the evaluation to be conducted in the clinical setting or the family's house, or a combination?; (3) comprehensiveness of the evaluation—How much information and understanding needs to be gathered before it is deemed enough to begin treatment and direct intervention; and (4) resources needed—What resources, human and otherwise, will be required for the evaluation process? (The entire nuclear family plus extended? friends? standardized tests? audio and video tape equipment?)

As those who are going to conduct evaluations resolve questions such as those identified above, a particular format they can be comfortable with will begin to emerge. The author would like to describe an evaluation format/process that has been successfully employed for sometime now with families where alcoholism is presenting a problem.

AN EVALUATION FORMAT/PROCESS

The following will present one perspective with regards to what constitutes an appropriate family evaluation when alcohol is prominently present. The readers must keep in mind their particular styles and orientations if they attempt to replicate this format. There may be particular types of information, or means of gathering the same, that would be considered more appropriate for their purposes. For the staff who employ this particular format it has been determined to be appropriate and valuable (Clinical Services Center, University of Wisconsin-Stout, Menomonie, Wisconsin). The overall format to be described at this time is usually completed in about a three-week period of time and, while regarded as systematically applied, there must be room for molding to meet what each family presents in its own idiosyncratic way.

Intake

When accepting the intake we are interested in primarily bio-data type of information: the name, address, phone number, and birth date of the person calling plus names and ages of other family members. Along with this data we need a brief description of the referring person's perception of the "problem" and any indication of prior treatments. We do not encourage long discourses on the telephone, as this may result in the referring person believing they have more of an alliance with the Center staff than what is the case. By promoting this perception on their part, we believe it is unfair to them and the rest of the family. We also make a practice, at the time of first contact with the whole family, of giving an overview to everyone regarding what was shared by the referring person on the phone. We believe this communicates to the family unit that we do not encourage or foster secrets and this spreads what attachment there may have been perceived as being between the Center staff and referring person into the whole family.

FLOW CHART

FAMILY EVALUATION PROCEDURE

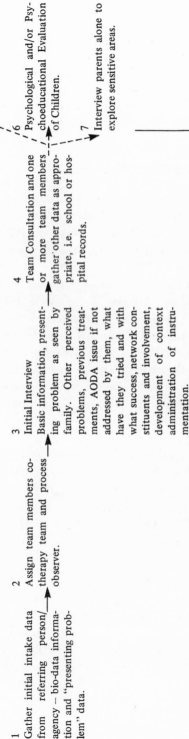

5
Home visit by team

6
Psychological and/or Psychoeducational Evaluation of Children.

7
Interview parents alone to explore sensitive areas.

4
Team Consultation and one or more team members gather other data as appropriate, i.e. school or hospital records.

3
Initial Interview
Basic information, presenting problem as seen by family. Other perceived problems, previous treatments, AODA issue if not addressed by them, what have they tried and with what success, network constituents and involvement, development of context administration of instrumentation.

2
Assign team members co-therapy team and process observer.

1
Gather initial intake data from referring person/agency – bio-data information and "presenting problem" data.

8
Family Task Session
Various tasks assigned and family conducts while observed and evaluated according to family system criteria (Lewis, et al. 1976).

9
Team Member Staffing
Share impressions and develop rough draft of report and recommendations – contact referral person to arrange exit interview.

10
Final Interview
Evaluation team, family, referral person (s). Impressions are shared along with recommendations (testing data).

11
Written Report and recommendations provided family and referral as permitted and appropriate.

——— solid line connecting components indicates always part of the evaluation

------- hyphenated line connecting components indicates optional part of the evaluation according to result of components 3 and 4.

When scheduling a family for an evaluation, it is standard practice to communicate over the telephone the purpose of the evaluation and what this typically entails operationally. This seems important to reduce the possibility of their thinking that a therapeutic contract is now in place as a result of their telephone call and then becoming disappointed and prematurely terminating.

Assign Team Members

Each evaluation team has three team members assigned to it. We like to have the team comprised of a male and female clinician to conduct the evaluation directly with the family. The third member can be of either sex, and it is their role to operate behind the one-way glass and be the "observer." There are times when one or more family members will be asked to go on the other side of the one-way mirror and observe the third team member.

The male-female team is valuable because of the symbolic fashion in which they represent a marital dyad as discussed by both Napier and Whitaker (1978) and Rubinstein and Weiner (1967). Frequently one or the other of the spouses, or the children, are more comfortable with a particular sex than the other, and the presence of a male-female team provides them with a readily available object for their positive transference.

Minuchin and Montalvo (1967) have discussed the value of having various family members observe the rest of the family interacting with others. This is particularly valuable when one-way glass is utilized and their observation is facilitated by a professional staff member. This procedure can often result in the "observing family member" being promoted to perceive other family members in an entirely different fashion from what has been previously believed.

Initial Interview

This first interview can last anywhere from one to two and one-half hours depending upon the size of the family unit and how quickly and effectively all those involved are able to work together. While the information gathered in the session will now be presented in a sequential fashion, it does not generally occur in this order. We believe the information to be valuable and use it as a framework for the first session, but generally find that the information is gathered in a different order each time, depending upon the interactive styles of the family and clinicians.

After reviewing the content of the referral telephone call, we will ask the family for their perception of what is "problematic," along with identifying what is is that they are interested in changing. This also provides a good opportunity for beginning to assess the way in which the various family members are mobilized around the problem, i.e. who's in alliance with whom. How calcified do the alliances appear to be? What affect is attached to the problem and alliances observed?

After identifying the problem, it is a natural step to determining what they have attempted to do to change or resolve it. As Weakland and his colleagues (1974) have identified, it seems so often peoples' attempted solutions to a problem are just what result in problem maintenance. An example of this would be the wife who manifests numerous behaviors to curb her husband's drinking, all of which simply serve to continue to enable him. By knowing what they have already attempted, we can avoid attempting the same things as well as develop a sense of their creative, problem-solving ability. This will also be the element used to determine what other human services they are, or have, utilized as a means of resolving their concerns. Frequently, we have found there were many services enlisted by a family, but there was no coordinated effort to insure a synergistic effect from their various offerings.

In this session, we are also interested in acquiring a vocational, educational, and medical history. We are aware of the reciprocal role of a checkered employment history or serious medical problems in the development of alcoholism and, for this reason, are interested in this information. The educational history is valuable in that this may be an area of enhancement that the adult members have overlooked as possibly being changed. If this is the case, one of the evaluation recommendations may revolve about facilitating their becoming involved in continuing education with the Division of Vocational Rehabilitation's assistance. We have frequently been impressed with how often the families are unaware of various resources that exist to provide assistance to those in need, such as themselves.

A typical spin-off from gathering this information is the issue of drinking history and role of the same in this family. While we utilize both the Michigan Alcoholism Screening Test (MAST) and the Minnesota Multiphasic Personality Inventory (MMPI) to assist in identifying alcoholic tendencies, our primary focus of attention is upon the family member's perceptions of alcohol in the family as a problem. We maintain that if someone is bothered or disturbed by the drinking, it is a problem in the relationship and in need of being contended with. In this session, our primary concern is with an assessment of the magnitude of the problem, its disruptive influence upon the family, and possible consequences (Davis et al. 1974).

As Davis and his colleagues have said: "Usually, in spite of the agreement by all of how terrible drinking is, the drinking pattern continues with a concomitant increase of feelings of frustration on everybody's part. Care must be taken to avoid this trap and to concentrate during the history-taking and clinical observation on what is adaptive about the drinking" (Davis, Berenson, Steinglass, and Davis, 1974, p. 210). By "adaptive" they do not intend to convey a sense of "goodness" or any other moral value. Rather, what they mean to communicate is that the drinking behavior may be resulting in some reinforcement or gain for the individuals involved and, if this is so, to determine these adaptive consquences could have considerable value in the treatment process. Three examples of possible "adaptive consequences" of drinking may be: (1) it allows an otherwise fight phobic couple to express aggression; (2) the drinking promotes a couple relating sexually by reducing her inhibitions and allowing him to avoid the experience of guilt about his extramarital affair; and (3) the drinking "allows" the father to become openly affectionate not only with his children, but his wife as well.

A brief family/marital history is also gathered in order to evaluate what, if any, developmental stressors (birth, death, loss of employment, geographical moves, etc.) may have disrupted the family's functioning in such a fashion that they are still attempting to accommodate to its effects. We are also interested in becoming aware of prior marriages and to what extent unresolved discord from those relationships may be taxing this unit. This is also a time when a determination will be made regarding what is the role of in-laws or other extended family in the family's functioning. Along with blood relatives, we are interested in determining the involvement of any others (neighbors, fellow employees, church members, etc.) in the family's life. If it is determined that others are extensively involved we will often either have them in for the second session or recommend the family engage the significant others in therapeutic efforts on a post-evaluation basis.

An assessment of what resources the family perceive as having available can be very important. This not only identifies for the team what is available for post-evaluation treatment efforts, but also assesses the family's level of general awareness regarding what the community and society does provide for their assistance.

This session is generally ended by asking the adult members to complete both the MAST and MMPI. Both the MAST and MMPI are used as a guide in determining the likelihood of alcoholism being present, and the MMPI is helpful in adding another dimension to the evaluation team's perception of them both intra and interpersonally.

Team Consultation and Retrieval of Information

After the initial interview the team consults with one another to share perceptions and determine what other information may need to be gathered. If there have been prior treatments or hospitalizations which seem significant, the records will be retrieved with the family's permission. If one or more children are having school difficulties, it is not unusual for a representative of the team to contact the school for their perceptions. At this time ideas are also generated with regards to what would be the most appropriate type of tasks to ask the family to engage in during the next session. A decision also needs to be made by the team regarding the advisability of using one or more of the evaluation processes, the three optional components which will be explained below.

Home Visit

Bloch (1973) has described the value of a home visit in facilitating the clinician's development of a more comprehensive perspective of the family. While a pragmatic concern, such as time available to the evaluation team, needs to be considered, we have found this to be a valuable component to the evaluation in most cases where it was utilized. This can greatly enhance the team's perception of how the space available to the family may constrain and compound their situation. Just as a house's physical layout molds and shapes human interaction, it is also true that the human responses can shape and affect the house's impact upon those present. An example of this would be the parents who are obviously without any means of gaining privacy for sexual functioning, or the seven-year-old who is relegated to a corner for his sleeping area while others have more accommodating situations. While this may be threatening to the clinicians to leave their "turf," most frequently it is a very rewarding venture.

In conducting a home visit, it is important for the clinicians to disqualify themselves as "honored guests." There is need to emphasize that this visit is designed to facilitate the evaluation and the development of a better understanding of them. As an honored guest you are not encouraged to tour the house, but as a clinician this needs to be identified as a prerogative. What can be particularly valuable is for one team member to receive a conducted tour by the children while the other team member converses with the parents. The conversation that accompanies the children's tour can often prove to be exceptionally enlightening. Access to intimate areas, such as the medicine cabinet, is important. Just as in a thorough medical examination, the clinician conducting a home visit must attempt to acquire access to the entire "body."

The home visit will generally be conducted if the family offers information that suggests their physical setting is significantly involved in their problems and/or if the evaluation team believes it would assist the family in feeling more comfortable in the evaluation context. Occasionally the visit will be conducted because the family extends the invitation.

Psychological/Psychoeducational Screening of Family Members

If it is determined from the evaluation process that one or more family members reportedly are having idiosyncratic, individual problems, the evaluation team will request an individual psychological or psychoeducational screening. The clinic psychological staff are utilized for these screenings. It is important to emphasize that these are brief screenings, as opposed to more exhaustive evaluations. As a result of the screening, a more thorough individual workup may be suggested by the screening clinician. The results of these screenings are then shared in the final interview, along with appropriate suggestions, by the clinician who conducted the screening. These screenings are most often conducted with the children of referred families when there is a history of marital/family turmoil, and it is the perception of the evaluation team members that it would be advisable.

Parents Seen Alone

When the team members believe it would be valuable to see the parents alone they will request this option. This decision is made on the basis of consideration of variables such as a couple's obvious uneasiness with discussing intimate areas of their relationship such as sex or various experiences that are too guilt inducing for them to discuss in the children's presence. There are also times, when due to a factor such as an extremely fused relationship between mother and a child, that the couple is unable to effectively be engaged with one another in the session, then a session with them alone is scheduled. Some parents also effectively occupy themselves with the comforts of their children to the degree that the session is not productive. If it appears that the couple, or one member of the couple, is effectively "hiding" via the children's presence, a session with the marital dyad alone will be scheduled.

Family Task Session

Prior to this session, the team evaluates their perceptions of the family and arrives at appropriate tasks to assign the family during this time. There are many tasks available for assignment (see "Evaluation Techniques" section of this chapter), but it is important that whatever is assigned is done so on the basis of evaluating what is known about the particular family. For instance, if the family appears to be particularly adroit at using words to hide behind, the clinicians may decide to assign tasks that do not allow the use of words such as family sculpting or drawing. If the family seems to have particular difficulty in making decisions, the task assigned may direct them to decide something so that the team might observe how they "break down" in their decision-making process.

During this phase of the evaluation, many other dimensions of the family as a system (as described in Chapters Two and Three) are noted. Patterns of interaction can often be observed when assigning tasks that involve decision making. Certainly the whole idea of "silencing mechanisms" (Zuk, 1975) are crucial for consideration here. Zuk has described kinds of observations the clinician may want to make in the presence of silencing mechanisms:

> He (therapist) wants to see and hear the process erupt before him; that is, to be in its presence when it occurs and if necessary be the spur for its occurrence. He wants to observe the response of the so-called victim. Does the victim fall silent or explode with rage? Does he plead with his silencers or castigate them? Does he show somatic symptoms such as flushing or trembling? Or does he show such inappropriate behavior as silly smiling, giggling, or laughter? (Zuk, 1975, p. 15).

Styles of communication are also crucial to observe at this juncture. Style of communication is here defined as how something is talked about by the participants, i.e. friendly, sociable, blaming, attacking, placating, etc. Miller, Nunnally and Wackman (1977) have described styles of communication in a very clear and concise fashion. Along with their description they have said the following, which underscores the importance of a person's style of communication: "Most partners think they can change the nature of their discussion simply by shifting their focus, by changing what they talk about. While changing what you talk about has an impact, your messages are most dramatically changed by shifting style; by shifting *how* you talk about something" (Miller, Nunnally and Wackman, 1977, p. 173). How is it that the people in this family talk with one another is crucial to the family with an alcoholic. The author has found that frequently the chronic prominence of affect in their relationship has resulted in their way of communicating with one another, becoming very calcified over the years. As calcified as it has become, they are equally unaware of it. The husband who responds in a sharp defensive pattern, and the wife who communicates her messages in a blaming and attacking fashion, as the oldest child communicates messages in a placating-pleading fashion are all similarly obvious to *how* they are communicating in such a fashion that they all continue to be locked into these "styles" and the resultant discomfort. It is as though they are lodged into these styles, and while their words say one thing, the way in which the message is conveyed communicates an opposite message to what the words logically convey. This incongruency in messages is not productive for any of the participants, as has been discussed by Bandler, Grinder, and Satir (1976).

As the family becomes involved in whatever the task may be there is also appropriate opportunity to observe what, if any, difference is allowed and/or promoted. Can differences in perceptions and beliefs be tolerated or is this another way in which people are squelched from developing in the family? If differences are not tolerated, in what way are people "put back in their place?" How is control exerted, and by whom, in order to maintain the "group think?" The author has observed that the family with an alcoholic frequently has extreme difficulty in allowing differences among its members. There seems to be a collective family mythology that defines themselves as being in such a chaotic and fragile way that differences are too threatening to allow to emerge.

During this session we have found the utilization of the *Beavers-Timberlawn Family Evaluation Scale* to be extremely helpful in organizing our perceptions of the family as a system (Lewis, J.M. et al., 1976). This scale provides fine point rating scales for fourteen different dimensions of family functioning. Through the utilization of these scales, a more systematic, and we believe comprehensive, perspective of the family is gathered. The fourteen dimensions of family functioning assessed are as follows:

1. *OVERT POWER.* This scale assesses issues of leadership, authority, control, and interpersonal influence.
2. *PARENTAL COALITION.* The parental relationship is assessed with regards to its apparent strength or weakness, considering both the mode of operation and the emotions present.
3. *CLOSENESS SCALE.* This scale is designed to look at boundaries that are operational in the family. The range is from those families with distinct boundaries and high levels

of closeness, those with distinct boundaries and great interpersonal distance, and those families with vague and indis-
tinct boundaries among members.

4. *FAMILY MYTHOLOGY.* How much congruence is there
between how the family perceives and defines itself and the
perceptions of those outside the family.

5. *GOAL-DIRECTED NEGOTIATION.* This variable refers
to ways in which a family solves problems.

6. *CLARITY OF EXPRESSION.* This scale ranges from communications that are very clear to those unintelligible, in-
concise.

7. *RESPONSIBILITY.* To what degree do the family members accept responsibility for individual actions, feelings,
and thoughts is the question pursued. In the families with
an alcoholic, we frequently observe denial and projection of
responsibility, just as is often identified as being characteristic of the alcoholic as an individual.

8. *INVASIVENESS.* Intrusions, invasions, or "mind reading"
(one person telling another member what that other member thinks or feels) are examples of behaviors evaluated in
this dimension.

9. *PERMEABILITY.* The degree to which the family acknowledges the messages from the members is assessed at
this point.

10. *RANGE OF FEELINGS.* The question explored here is
how wide a spectrum of emotions does this family experience and communicate. So often these families are observed
to be constricted and "emotionally strangled."

11. *MOOD AND TONE.* The family's basic or most pervasive
mood is measured in this scale, e.g., warm, polite, hostile,
depressed, pessimistic, or other primary moods.

12. *UNRESOLVABLE CONFLICT.* Whether or not, or to
what degree, can this family deal with conflict is assessed via
consideration of this dimension. As Lewis and his colleagues reported, it seems that effectiveness in dealing with
conflict is a far more important variable than how much is
experienced.

13. *EMPATHY SCALE.* To what degree can family members
respond to each other's feelings with understanding?

14. *GLOBAL HEALTH-PATHOLOGY.* The overall level of

competence of this family, in light of all the dimensions, is assessed in this final scale.

By utilizing this scale, we have found that it is far less likely that we might overlook a particular dimension of family functioning. It is not complex to use and serves as an excellent cognitive map for organizing the observation of a family and resultant data. Without the aid of this scale, or something similar to it, it is far too easy to get caught up in listening to the content or "story-telling" and lose sight of the process dimensions which are so crucial.

This session, like the first, may take from one to two hours, depending again upon number of members in the family and their characteristic relationship styles. At the end of this session, the third and last session will be scheduled for the evaluation process.

Team Member Staffing

This component of the procedure is crucial. The three team members meet to share impressions again and analyze all of the various data gathered. A primary concern in this process is that the observations identified to be written and then shared with the family can be translated into a "plan of action for change" should the family opt for treatment on a post-evaluation basis. Along with the analysis of the data gathered, consideration is also given to whom ever else should be involved in the exit interview. For instance, if an alcohol and drug abuse counselor made the referral and has been extensively involved with one or more of the family members, we will frequently invite him to sit in. Another example would be a social worker from the county social service department who made the referral and will continue to be involved with the family. Of course, a release from the family needs to be acquired, but this has not been a problem.

As usual, the team will get the report typed up in rough draft form so that they might refer to it with the family in the final session. A rough draft is used because other new ideas may be generated and then incorporated into the final draft in the last session.

The format for this report begins with basic bio-data information regarding the family, i.e., names, birthdates, address, etc.

This is then followed by identification of reason for the referral and/or presenting problem. The "background" section follows and closely approximates what is typically defined as a social history. In this section, marital, medical, and vocational history is covered along with other information, such as prior treatments and outside resources perceived to be available to the family.

The next section is titled "Individual Descriptions" and is just that. Each individual in the family is described according to the perceptions of the clinicians involved and whatever psychological testing has been conducted.

The section to follow, "Family Description," presents how the individuals just described appear to work as a family. While this is the longest section of the report, it is perceived as a really crucial one as far as intervention is concerned. If any one section could be defined as the core or heart component of the overall evaluation, this would be it.

The next section is titled "AODA Issue" and refers to the nature and degree of the alcohol or other drug abuse problem present in this family. Along with the family's perceptions, the Michigan Alcoholism Screening Test and Minnesota Multiphasic Personality Inventory are utilized for assistance in this matter.

The last section is a "Summary and Recommendation." The report is briefly summarized and followed by appropriate recommendations for consideration by the famiy. As mentioned before, the recommendations are made with ease of implementation in mind. To illustrate this, consider one case of a couple with two young children who had been referred as a result of the wife's involvement with an outpatient alcohol and other drug abuse counselor for after care on a post-hospitalization basis. Both of the adults had been married before, and each had brought one child to this marriage from a prior union. Also, both of the partners had been through inpatient treatment; she has maintained sobriety for a period of one year; he is still using drugs occasionally, but with far more control than ever before. The referral was stimulated by a child's self-destructive behavior. The following constitute the recommendations that evolved from their involvement in the evaluation process.

In light of the above report, the following recommendations are offered.

1. A case management staffing be conducted including the family and

human service professionals who are presently involved with them in order to coordinate and consolidate treatment in line with the family's expressed desires and goals.

2. Family therapy be engaged in for the purposes of:

  a. addressing the marital issues that Matt and Jayne have identified as possible areas for change

  Matt—

  —his impulsive behavior

  —becoming a more supportive and attentive spouse

  —becoming more responsible for self

  —becoming a more active parent including providing Jayne with more time alone

  —his blaming of Jayne's parents

  —his providing more physical contact within their relationship

  Jayne—

  —responsibility for self through more direct and assertive communication of feelings and needs;

  —redefining her role with her parents;

  —cooperating and supporting Matt in his attempt to be more responsible for self by doing less nagging and believing more in him.

  b. Strengthening Matt and Jayne's parental dyad, which would occur in conjunction with strengthening of the marital dyad.

  c. To assist the group in developing their identity as a group and to promote a sense of wholeness for themselves as a family unit.

  d. To assist Jayne in clarifying boundaries between herself as an individual, and her parents; to establish and clarify more productive boundaries between Matt and Jayne and Jayne's parents. It would be more productive to begin this work with Jayne and her parents alone.

  e. To provide Matt and Jayne with appropriate child management techniques, which they would be responsible for consistently applying.

  f. To facilitate them learning how to provide more time for themselves as a marital unit within the environmental constraints they have.

3. It is deemed appropriate for clinicians to continue providing play therapy and other related services for Tim. To facilitate Clare's accommodation to the changes the family is involved in, similar services seem appropriate for her.

4. That both Matt and Jayne continue in their after-care programming from the inpatient AODA treatment. This primarily consists of regular AA meetings at present.

The above recommendations are characteristic of many families with an alcoholic member. The first recommendation concerned itself with all of the various helpers that had become involved in these people's lives. While there is no doubt that all were well intentioned, there were obvious situations where some were working at cross purposes to others. Also, these people were literally being "meetinged to death." There was hardly a spare moment in their schedules as they went from agency to agency. This was in need of monitoring and being better coordinated than what was the case.

A few of the other recommendations appear worthy of further comment, while the rest remain self-explanatory. Recommendation 2 had to do with clarifying boundaries between Jayne, as an individual, and her parents. Until this individuation process was culminated, it seemed apparent that she would continue to perceive herself in this "loyalty bind" between her parents and Matt. She felt in a bind and as though, regardless of who she turned to, she would be in trouble. It was suggested that this individuation process commence between Jayne and her parents without Matt being initially present. There was considerable animosity between her parents and Matt, and much of this seemed attributable to her parent's extensive "emotional invest-ment" in her and resultant difficulty in allowing her to enter this marriage with another man. As this component of the treatment progressed, Matt was brought into these sessions. This could only be accomplished after Jayne and her parents were able to disengage so that the parents did not define her marriage as testimony of her lack of loyalty to them. Also Jayne and Matt had developed a more firm sense of their own marriage and no longer responded as defensively to the parents' emotion, which did nothing more than intensify and calcify their reaction.

Recommendation 3 had to do with the treatment Tim (Matt's son from an earlier marriage) was receiving. Tim had been very much identified as a problem while Jayne's daughter, Clare (also from a prior marriage), was defined as the good one. Our concern was that the play therapy could be defined in such a way that Tim would be locked into the role of the "sick one" in comparison to Clare. For this reason we recommended that Clare also receive play therapy "to facilitate Clare's accommodation to the changes the family is involved in." Our concern was to take the sting out of the play therapy as a means of defining someone as "sick" and rather as defining it as "an aid to fostering normal development." Clare would be able to benefit from this relationship in that she was a shy, withdrawn five-year-old who had a very strong attachment to her mother. We thought, if nothing else, this would facilitate her detaching from mother to start school the following fall. Also, as Matt and Jayne began to develop a more productive and mutually rewarding relationship, there was the possibility that Clare could feel rejected, so the play therapy provided her with a new and special relationship which was "all her own."

Final Interview

As previously mentioned, this session is attended by the family members, clinicians who conducted the evaluation, and any significant others, such as referral persons. This will generally take from sixty to ninety minutes.

The primary goal is to share with the family the perceptions of the evaluation team along with resultant recommendations. This provides the family the opportunity to validate, or invalidate, the team's perceptions. In all cases (where recommendations suggest it) the family is assisted in identifying how they might go about accomplishing what has been recommended. This may range from contracting with them for family therapy, to identifying inpatient alcohol and other drug abuse treatment units, to how to contact the Division of Vocational Rehabilitation and identifying services offered there, to educational remediation for the children.

Final Written Report

The team once again assembles to determine what modifications, if any, are mandated for inclusion in the final report as a result of the final session. Once the final report is developed, a copy is sent to the referral person (as appropriate) and a copy of the recommendations is sent to the family for their further consideration.

SUMMARY

This chapter was designed to describe the family evaluation process developed by the author at the University of Wisconsin-Stout's Clinical Service Center. This procedure was initially designed for utilization with families where one or more of the members is suspected of being alcoholic. The chapter opened with an identification of the rationale for this evaluation process and was followed by the description of various family evaluation techniques that have been described in the literature. From this point, discussion focussed on what one perceived as important theoretical considerations to be considered by those who might engage in family evaluations. The evaluation procedures developed by the author were then described, with case data presented for purposes of illustration, as deemed appropriate.

Chapter 7

ALCOHOL AND SEX

THE author would like to begin this chapter with a quote regarding alcohol consumption offered by Shakespeare in his play *Macbeth*: "it provokes the desire, but it takes away the performance." Throughout man's history the myth that "spirits" will result in heightened sexual activity and enjoyment has entrapped people. Too many people believe alcohol to be a sexual stimulant. While it is known that reduction of inhibitions occurs with alcohol ingestion, we also know that the body function is depressed and actually interferes with performance. Alcohol, as a depressant, actually blocks the neural pathways that govern erection and sexual responsiveness, and thus causes temporary, secondary impotence. Masters and Johnson (1970) have determined that prolonged and excessive use of alcohol can result in damage to the central nervous system and lead to irreversible, permanent sexual impotence, even into sobriety. The incidence of impotence among male alcoholics is 10 percent or higher, which is reversible in about half of the cases, the ability to reverse the condition is primarily dependent upon the neurological damage incurred (*NIAAA/IFS*, Sept. 20, 1978, p. 5). Female alcoholics frequently report frigidity and/or lack of vaginal lubrication. Like the male's impotence, both of these conditions can most frequently be reversed with sobriety and treatment.

While this chapter will address various of the specific sexual dysfunctions and their treatment, the most pervasive, single, etiological factor for sexual dysfunctions with the alcoholic is the inability to form intimate relationships (Howard and Howard, 1978; and Forrest, 1978). Dr. Charles L. Whitfield, of the University of Maryland School of Medicine, has said: "The most nt sexual problem in alcoholics is the inability to form intimate relationships" (*NIAAA/IFS*, Sept. 20, 1978, p. 5). When there is a problem in forming, and developing, relationships it is to be expected that there will be sexual difficulties. The old cliche, "when there are problems in the living room, there are bound to be problems in the bedroom," is full of sound wisdom. If the partners are experiencing feelings such as hurt, rejection, anger, being untrusted, and deceived, it is unlikely that a flourishing sexual relationship is going to be reported. As the relationship begins, and is then gradually eroded as a result of the drinking and concomitant behaviors that generate feelings such as those just identified, it would be unusual to find the relationship where sexual activity is both frequent and satisfying to both partners. In one report, regarding a treatment program for married alcoholics, which included the nonalcoholic spouse, it was found that whether male or female, alcoholic or not, all involved reported feelings of sexual inadequacy and failure (Strack and Dutton, 1971). Perhaps it should be mentioned that sexual problems are prominent in marriages where alcohol is not a problem as well. In one extensive study (DeBurger, 1975) it was reported that 25 percent of those seeking help for their marriages identified maladjustment in sexual relationships as their primary difficulty. In an earlier study, Ellis (1969) reported that 94 percent of couples seen by him indicated sexual dissatisfaction was one of the problems in their marriage.

The author's experience has suggested that difficulty in the area of sexual functioning is one which is to be expected in almost 100 percent of the relationships where alcohol is a problem. Sex and alcohol are not "strange bedfellows," but rather "volatile bedfellows." When addressing groups of alcoholic couples, and beginning to approach the area of sexuality, this is typically a time when eyes are turned toward the floor, faces flush, and bodies are nervously readjusted in their chairs. The author believes these behavioral manifestations are not just recognition reflexes acknowledging an area where difficulty resides, but also reflective of the general anxiety and discomfort which is attached to sex in their relationships. Renshaw (LoPiccolo and LoPiccolo, 1978) has identified three important A's in the etiology of impotence (broadly used to refer to male and female sexual arousal), namely, alcohol, anxiety, and anger. She indicates that both anxiety and anger are mediated through the sympathetic nervous system, and when activated, counter relaxation (parasympathetic dominance), and the sexual response. The anger of the old-remembered conflicts, cutting remarks, and perhaps physical abuse, along with the anxiety from the uncertainty of the relationship and past sexual frustrations, all culminate in sexual dysfunction.

These three A's become involved in a very destructive and self-perpetuating vicious cycle. The more alcohol that is consumed, the more difficult it becomes to perform adequately. As the male experiences erectile failure more and more frequently, he becomes more and more anxious, which lessens the likelihood of his developing and maintaining an erection. In order to protect his own fragile and threatened sense of masculinity he cuts his wife with hurtful remarks, and she becomes angry and likewise feeds into his anxiety and anger, which makes it unlikely either of them are going to be able to be sexually responsive. As Howard and Howard have stated: "Most problem drinkers have learned during their late teens and early twenties to use alcohol to relieve anxieties" (1978, p. 157). So with the anxiety and anger, the husband turns to the "problem solver" of most familiarity—the alcohol—and continues the destructive cycle identified as the "Three A's." Each such inconclusive and unpleasant encounter further undermines the relationship and reduces the likelihood of satisfying sexual contact.

As this cycle repeats itself over time it becomes paradoxically more difficult for the couple to do what is so essential: to talk about their frustrations. As has been said by the authors of *The Dilemma of the Alcoholic Marriage* about the couple discussing sexual issues:

> It (sex) is so highly charged with emotions of one sort or another —guilt, resentment, bitterness, love—that a reasonable exchange of views and grievances may be virtually impossible. A talk may start out calmly, but as soon as one or the other accuses or reproaches, tempers flare, along with the determination to retaliate. Nothing can be accomplished in this way, which may explain why people give up before they start talking things out and dismiss the whole business with: "Let's not talk about it" (Alanon Family Group Headquarters, 1971, p. 40).

This "Let's not talk about it" attitude does nothing more than result in festering of the old wounds regarding this component of their relationship. Just as Cadogan (1979) has reported, it has been this author's experience that facilitating communication between the partners regarding their sexual relationship frequently results in quick turnabouts. As the couple discusses their sexual fears, expectancies, and beliefs, they become able to better understand one another and themselves as sexual beings and what they might do to best insure more satisfying sexual contact in the future. A crucial element of this facilitated interaction consists of encouraging both to own what they have disowned of themselves and projected onto the other. The projection process, as used here, consists of denying, displacing, and projecting onto the other a trait of one's self, which arouses anxiety and/or is inconsistent with one's self-perception. An example of this would be the alcoholic husband who experiences erectile failure with his wife and finds this threatening to his masculine self-image. The way he handles this experience, which is uncomfortable for him, is to project it out onto his wife and accuse her of being frigid and/or sexually not exciting. Through encouraging them to begin to communicate about their sexual difficulties, the road to a new relationship is paved. As Hanson and Estes have said: "When two people experience mutual respect and freedom to disclose themselves in the presence of the other without contrivance, sexual activity thrives. . . . In the presence of alcoholism, couples experience minimal opportunity for spontaneous sharing, since each is continually on guard for fear of being hurt by the other" (1977, p. 70).

Hanson and Estes state that the potential for spontaneous sharing is blocked in the presence of alcoholism, and this is the reason the author, and others (Forrest, 1978; LoPiccolo and LoPiccolo, 1978), believe that the drinking problem needs to be assessed and addressed before dealing therapeutically with the sexual problem(s). LoPiccolo and LoPiccolo explicitly state that sex therapy is contraindicated until drinking has been controlled for six months. This author believes treatment of sex problems can begin sooner than what the LoPiccolo's suggest, but is continuously cognizant of the effect of continued drinking on sexual functioning. One's concern is not only with the physiological impact of alcohol on sexual functioning, but also the probability of blockage to intimate sharing, verbally and otherwise, by the couple. Again and again the author has had nonalcoholic spouses report to him that it was at least two years of sobriety or controlled drinking before they really began to be as trusting of their alcoholic mate as they once were. Considering these dimensions, it seems precipitous to begin direct intervention with sexual problems until the drinking problem is checked or well on its way to being resolved.

Before moving into the area of treatment of sexual dysfunctions in the alcoholic relationship, the author would like to express some of what is known about etiology of sexual dysfunctions in both male and female alcoholics/problem drinkers. The author believes that being aware of what is known about the two sexes can be very facilitative to the treatment process. Just as Master's and Johnson (1970) have determined that lack of information, and/or misinformation, is a prominent etiological factor in human sexual dysfunctions, the author believes lack of information or knowledge by the counselor of those being treated can also be problematic.

MALE ALCOHOLICS AND SEXUALITY

Males in our society are frequently expected to be aggressive and devoid of feelings, both of which are prominent characteristics of alcoholic males and those with sexual dysfunction. If a male has a comfortable perception and integration of his aggressiveness, it is likely he will be able to participate in a mutual give-and-take sexual relationship. If the male is also able to be comfortable with and both express and receive his feelings he is also even more likely to be able to develop and maintain a mutually satisfying sexual relationship. All too often though, what is observed is the male alcoholic who portrays himself as the "Macho Man," inferring he is aggressive and domineering and also callous to his partner's feelings (and probably his own as well).

Part of the male's sex role in our society is that he is to be a sex expert. It is not at all uncommon to hear men report that they believe women expect them to know "everything about sex." When they are first confronted with "failure" (usually nothing out of the ordinary as far as sexual functioning is concerned, such as momentary erectile failure or the female partner not achieving orgasm) his self-image is damaged and he comes to fear "failure," which is almost certain to result in the self-fulfilling prophecy in the form of erectile failure or some other dysfunction. Supposedly he is to "know it all" and cannot admit concern, so he goes deeper and deeper into anxiety and self-trepidation, worsening his situation. It is not uncommon for this situation to lead to depression, so he reaches to alcohol to "loosen up" and finds his situation now even more confounded. The performance demand continues to haunt him (by tradition of the Protestant work ethic, the male's happiness is tied directly to industriousness) and leads to a vicious cycle with a downward spiral. In many ways he has become a spectator of his sexual being, and spontaniety is gone. The more he expects and demands of himself sexually, the more he fails to succeed, and the more depressed, anxious and drinking behavior manifested, the more he fails to experience success and the more he pushes himself, and so on. All this while he feels compelled to not talk about this internal experience because it is "not masculine." As Reed has said of men: "Since he has to be stoic at work and brave in sports, he is a combination of both in bed" (Reed, 1977, p. 213). So he goes on in his silent suffering and using the alcohol as an anesthetic to his fear, hurt, and anguish, all the while confounding his situation.

Another factor in need of consideration is the high proportion of alcoholics who come from families where one or both parents were alcoholic. Considering characteristics of alcoholic marriages it is not unrealistic to expect that males from these families did not observe their parents exchanging many affectionate behaviors. Masters and Johnson (1970), and others, have stated that comfort with one's own sexuality can be greatly enhanced by being able to observe one's parents being comfortable with affection between one another. Many adult male alcoholics probably did not have this demonstrated for them and, thus, are impoverished in the area of ability to emit affectionate behaviors and be comfortable with their own sexuality. In conjunction with this, males are not encouraged to do much physical touching from the time they enter adolescence. It should not be surprising, considering this point, that wives often report that their husbands do not engage in much touching in foreplay. This all culminates in a human being who is trained to be callous, "non-touching," "non-feeling," and a supposed "sex-pert" in the absence of sound information in most cases. Obviously, none of these characteristics are conducive to enhancing sexual functioning. What they are conducive to is loneliness, fear, despair, low self-esteem and self-worth, and alcoholism.

These are examples of the kinds of issues that must be addressed with the male alcoholic if sexual dysfunctions are to be reversed. To facilitate this change in the presence of the female partner can be vital in order to solicit her understanding and empathy as an ally. While it can be valuable to conduct a sexual history with each alone, it is essential to then bring them together and facilitate their learning and change process together.

FEMALE ALCOHOLICS AND SEXUALITY

"The female is often confused as to the meaning of her sexuality. She often questions herself and wonders if sex is for marriage, sex is for love, sex is for children, sex is for her own pleasure, sex is for acceptance, sex is for emotional security, sex is for physical release, or sex is for money. Rarely is she informed that her sexuality is an innate natural gift as are all other parts of her mind, body, and feelings" (Doyle, 1977, p. 238). As Doyle is describing the dilemma of many females in the population, his analysis seems particularly appropriate for most females with alcohol problems. For these women the sexual confusion probably only confounded their life and may have contributed to alcohol abuse, but is also confounding their present relationship and treatment efforts. A recent study (Beckman, 1979) seems to support this idea. Beckman's data suggested that one reason alcoholic females drank was to enhance their sexuality and sense of sexual adequacy. She concluded that alcohol was perceived by the women as a means of improving their sexual performance and/or the excessive drinking intensified sexual problems, which were then alleviated or denied by additional drinking. Beckman recommended, based upon her findings, that treatment programs should attempt to disrupt the cognitive link many women have between alcohol and improved sexual functioning. As this seems to be a valuable recommendation, it appears to be one worthy of implementing long before females find themselves in a treatment setting.

The dilemma of women and sexuality, identified by Doyle at the outset of this section, is even more intensified when we consider the often found childhood family environment of the female alcoholic. The typical constellation reported is that of a cold, distant mother and a warm affectionate father with whom the girl frequently identifies. Not only is there a void as far as an appropriate feminine model is concerned, but it is also likely that the child was not exposed to open displays of affection between mother and father, which Masters and Johnson (1970) have identified as so necessary to the development of a sense of wholesome sexuality. This likelihood is also suggested when we consider the far greater incidence of alcoholic fathers among a female alcoholic population. Schuckit (1972) determined that alcoholism in fathers of female alcoholics may be as high as 33 percent as compared to 7-8 percent in the mothers. The warmth between their fathers, and female alcoholics, is also reported as having often led to sexual intercourse or other overt sexual behavior. The implications of this type of behavior are naturally considerable on the young girls conception of sexuality and her own sense of feminine identity and relationships with males in general.

The author believes it is experiences such as these that result in the rage women alcoholics often manifest while intoxicated. The rage emanating from feeling cheated of an appropriate feminine model and not really being sure of how she is to relate to herself or others in her environment. While wanting to relate to women, she finds herself being more comfortable with men as a result of generalizing her own lack of a sense of value to women in general. As reported recently (*NIAAA/IFS*, September 20, 1978, p. 5), women alcoholics frequently do not wish to associate with women as much as men when they first achieve sobriety. This report indicates that this does not have so much to do with the alcoholism as it does with the woman not valuing herself as a woman. It seems she has the attitude that unless a man values her she is not valuable. This frequently observed phenomena has resulted in the perception that recovering alcoholic women have to work with their dependency on men as well as dependency on alcohol. In treatment settings it is often observed that women request a male sponsor and isolate themselves from other women with the statement, "I get along with men better."

Along with these observations there is then need to acknowledge the general social conditioning of women. As young males are reinforced for "getting it," young females are rewarded for "saving it." Sex is not as prominently present in the form of conversation even among young girls as compared to young boys. Girls also are recipients of many messages that convey to them that their genitalia are "dirty" or not as good as the "plumbing" of their young male counterparts. When we consider the prominence of sexually related concerns manifested by nonalcoholic women, it seems that we should not be surprised at the prominence of such concerns among the female alcoholic population.

In the report of a program for alcoholic women, the author had the following to say that seemed appropriate for consideration in understanding and treating the alcoholic female: "To ensure "proper" sex role identification, residents are assured by staff and peers that they are 'real' women who have the same needs, desires, and capacities to love and be loved as do their nonalcoholic sisters. Myths of the wanton female alcoholic are dispelled through heart to heart talks in which the women reveal themselves as isolated individuals with little desire for love and adventure" (Volpe, 1980, p. 44).

DISCUSSING SEXUAL MATTERS

Masters and Johnson (1970) have emphatically stated that there is no uninvolved partner in sexual dysfunction. They have suggested that it is far too easy to work with the "frigid" wife as the problem without any acknowledgment of how the husband reacts to her in order to maintain the "frigidity" and thereby protect himself from confronting his own sexual doubts and insecurities. In this same sense, there is a real danger in accepting the alcoholic spouse as the one with the sexual problem and lose sight of the relationship nature of sex. To be successful in intervening with a sexual dysfunction it seems imperative to involve both partners, particularly when one is alcoholic. The alcoholic spouse has probably become accustomed to blame, and without a concerted effort to understand the sexual difficulty as a relationship issue, it is likely the alcoholic will again accept/ solicit the blame.

It is likely that there will be significant misunderstanding regarding sexual functioning on the part of one or both partners. If blatant misinformation is not found, then it is likely there will be socially conditioned negative attitudes toward sex such as: the man who is found to subscribe to the belief that his partner should achieve orgasm every time or else he is a failure; the women who feels herself a failure if she does not achieve orgasm and arouse her partner; and, the woman who is fearful of communicating to her partner what she likes because she believes she would be perceived as "forward" or not a good sex partner because "women are to please men." While this is occurring for the woman, the man does not ask what she might like because "he is supposed to know." Examples such as these illustrate the reason that people soon come to feel paralyzed sexually. They come to perceive themselves as failures and adopt a "spectator role" where they maintain conscious control of their feelings and responses during sexual contact and amplify their lack of responsiveness and sense of failure. As Masters and Johnson have said: ". . . fear of inadequacy is the greatest known deterrant to effective sexual functioning, simply because it so completely distracts the fearful individual from his or her natural responsivity by blocking the reception of sexual stimuli" (1970, pp. 12-13).

In order to address the issue of the sexual component of a couple's relationship, helpers should be certain of possessing comfort with their own sexuality, along with a knowledge of the physiology of the human sexual response. Without these "tools" it is possible for the helper to confound the couple's difficulties by conveying improper information and attitudes either on an explicit or implicit level.

One way of communicating one's own comfort with sexuality is through the ease and fashion about which it is spoken. For some time there has been debate surrounding the use of earthy, slang words to discuss sex rather than the more formal anatomical jargon. This author believes it is a crucial issue that needs to be considered so that clients are not offended by discussing sex with someone who they perceive as not understanding them, and/or is not understandable. It seems that an effective way of working is to assess the vocabulary they use to discuss sex and initially join them at that level, gradually leading them to other utilization. This process becomes one of translating their terminology into the proper medical terms. Naturally this must be done sensitively so they do not feel condescended to, or ridiculed. The inherent value in this translating process is that slang words have potentially divergent meanings to people and may lead to tremendous misunderstanding. Slang words are also heavily ladened with emotional connotations that can be very destructive and counterproductive to the therapeutic process. The following is an example of the translation process being referred to. Therapist responding after one spouse has made it obvious that "it" is the term used to refer to intercourse. "So the frequency of it—intercourse—is something you would like changed. How often do the two of you have intercourse?" In the process of speaking these two sentences the translation has been made, and assuming the counselor has been comfortable and matter-of-fact in the presentation, a new level of comfort can be transmitted to the clients. If the medical terms are used in a stuffy and formal fashion, the chances are that the clients may come to perceive the therapist as alien to them and their style. The greater degree of specificity attached to medical words, along with the diminished emotionality when compared to that carried by slang words, can go far to enhance a couple's ability to begin to change the sexual component of their relationship. Again, though, it is important to emphasize the need for therapists to utilize their own therapeutic sensitivity and judgment in making the decision regarding when and how to use medical, sexual terminology.

SEXUAL DYSFUNCTIONS

An overview of some of the more common sexual dysfunctions are presented in this section. Readers who are interested in a more thorough discussion will find books by the following authors worthwhile: Belliveau and Richter, 1970; Kaplan, 1974; and Masters and Johnson, 1966 and 1970.

Premature ejaculation is one of the more common sexual dysfunctions presented in a treatment setting. There are basically two ways to define this difficulty. One way is to look upon the man's inability to delay ejaculation long enough for the woman to have orgasm 50 percent of the time. If the woman is unable to experience orgasm for reasons other than her partner's rapid ejaculation, this definition would not apply. Masters and Johnson (1970) use this definition because it considers satisfaction of both of the partners as the primary criteria. Others define premature ejaculation as an inability to delay ejaculating for thirty to sixty seconds after the penis is in the vagina. Regardless of which definition is utilized, premature ejaculation is the most common sexual dysfunction of men and also the most easily resolved through utilization of the squeeze technique (Kaplan, 1974). Primary prematurity refers to that condition where the male has never been able to control orgasm. Secondary prematurity describes that condition where the male developed a problem after a history of control.

Ejaculatory incompetence is the opposite of premature ejaculation. In this condition, the male is unable to ejaculate while the penis is contained in his partner's vagina. Most of these men can ejaculate through masturbation, or even fellatio, but have a mental block against allowing their seminal fluid to enter the vagina. In its milder forms, the male may only experience this difficulty in specific anxiety-provoking situations, such as when with a new partner or when he experiences guilt about the sexual encounter. Seldom is a physical-organic condition related to this dysfunction. Common explanations for this condition are a strict religious upbringing, suppressed anger, fear of abandonment, and/or ambivalence toward his partner. As with the premature ejaculator, the male with this dysfunction often anticipates failure and frustration, which compounds and often leads to the inability to maintain an erection.

Male impotence is that dysfunction described as the male being unable to develop and maintain an erection to allow penetration of the vagina, or of being unable to maintain his erection long enough after vaginal penetration to ejaculate. Primary impotence is characterized by that situation where the male has never been potent with a female, although he may be able to maintain an erection in other situations. The male who has functioned well prior to the onset of the impotence is characterized as experiencing secondary impotence. Fatigue, excessive drinking, undiagnosed diabetes, hepatitis, low androgen levels, depression, and guilt have all been linked to impotence in the male.

The reader will notice that as attention is turned to the more common female sexual dysfunctions, many of the same etiological sources are identified as were true for males. Belliveau and Richter (1970) seem to have caught the essence of the rationale for this:

> But what if a person has not had the opportunity or the information with which to construct a positive value system about sex? Worse yet, what if everything a child or young person growing up has heard or been taught about sex is negative? Of course, in these instances, the signals

from the psychosocial system will exert a negative influenc
functioning. Both sexes need positive signals from both sy
sexually capable. To this extent, the sexual problems of men a
have similar sources (p. 158).

Female orgasmic dysfunction is that situation where the woman is having difficulty experiencing an orgasm. This is probably the most common situation presented in the treatment of female alcoholics. Primary orgasmic dysfunction pertains to the woman who has never experienced an orgasm by any means. Women with secondary orgasmic dysfunction responded orgasmically at one time, but no longer are able to respond. Reasons offered for the presence of this condition are excessive and punitive religious beliefs; ambivalence or blatant dissatisfaction with her partner; marriage to a sexually inadequate male; and lack of sufficient emotional maturity to develop female identification and development of a functional sexual value system, which is so common for the female alcoholic.

Vaginismus is that condition where the female experiences an involuntary tightening or spasm in the outer third of the vagina, resulting in either a complete inability to be penetrated, or the woman experiences penetration, but only with considerable pain. Reasons for this dysfunction consist of fear of pain resultant from vaginal penetration, family background that associated sex with sin, a husband's impotence, psychological effects of rape, and more pervasive relationship problems. Physical problems that may result in vaginismus are a rigid hymen, inflammatory pelvic diseases and tumors, hemmorhoids, and childbirth pathologies. Of course, these are conditions that should be ruled out by the physician in a physical examination prior to sexual therapy with the couple where the female partner indicates vaginismus is a problem.

Dyspareunia (painful intercourse) and lack of erotic response to sexual stimulation is the last female sexual dysfunction to be mentioned. This condition is very commonly encountered in the treatment setting. In most cases a physical examination does not determine the cause. It seems that a combination of psychological and physiological events related to the attitude she holds toward the partner and herself are the primary instigators. The pain is usually caused by the lack of vaginal lubrication.

Vaginal lubrication is the female response to sexual stimulation that parallels the presence of an erection by the male. In the absence of vaginal lubrication, the women is probably neither physiologically nor psychologically ready for intercourse. Women plagued with this condition quite naturally derive little, if any, erotic pleasure from sexual stimulation. This dysfunction is most commonly associated, as one might guess, with the woman who has no affection, respect, or understanding for her partner and usually perceives none of these emanating from him. Fears such as pregnancy, pain, or inadequacy in the male may also precipitate this situation. Infection and physical conditions such as childbirth scars may also result in painful intercourse and the resultant resistance to sexual activities. Thinning of the vaginal walls, which is common in the fifty to seventy-year age group may also result in painful intercourse. The presence or absence of these conditions should be determined by physical examination.

Before leaving the overview of common sexual dysfunctions, it seems important to again emphasize a point. At no time in the previous discussion was lack of proper information or the presence of sexual misinformation specified as an etiological factor in sexual dysfunctions. In no way should this be interpreted to mean lack of information, or misinformation, is not a factor in sexual dysfunctions. In fact, the opposite is probably true. There is probably no more pervasive reason for the presence of sexual dysfunctions than lack of information or being misinformed. The author agrees wholeheartedly with Masters and Johnson's (1970) resolute assertion that ignorance, more than anything else, results in sexual dysfunction. It is for this reason that information about sexual functioning should assume a prominent role in sex therapy.

TREATMENT OF SEXUAL DYSFUNCTIONS

In treating the sexually dysfunctional relationship, it is helpful to conduct a brief history-taking process. One format suggested to follow is presented in the Group for Advancement of Psychiatry's book, *Assessment of Sexual Dysfunction* (1974). The areas this format attends to are childhood sexuality, adolescence, orgastic experiences, feelings about self as masculine or feminine, sexual fantasies and dreams, dating history, direct sexual experience with partners and other experiences (both pre/postmarital), and other information that seems appropriate to the couple. Examples of other information worth pursuing, depending upon the couple, are the exploration of effects and treatment of a rape, or pursuing thoughts and feelings surrounding a homosexual encounter one partner experienced some years ago. The determination of what to explore outside of this history format is determined by reactions of therapists to the couple as they present their histories in the clinical setting.

In the area of childhood sexuality, the following have proven to be valuable to determine: family attitudes about sex; how sex was learned about and from whom; childhood sex activity (sight of nude body, self-stimulation, and sexual exploration with another); childhood sexual myths; and any contact with the primal scene.

In exploring the period of adolescence, it is important to ascertain the following: preparation for adolescent physiological changes (who informed, nature of information, age at which received, and feelings regarding how the information was relayed); masturbatory activity; heterosexual contact; and homosexual encounters.

Orgastic experiences may be touched upon while explaining other areas already mentioned. Information clinically helpful to explore at this juncture, if not already covered with client, includes: frequency of orgasm during sleep and accompanying dreams; age and frequency of masturbation, along with feelings about and methods used to achieve orgasm; age when necking and petting were begun and with whom and how often; age at first intercourse and with whom and resultant feelings; and other coital experiences since the first encounter.

Regarding the individual's self-perceptions as masculine or feminine, it has proven useful to determine feelings about body size, appearance (handsome, etc.), voice, hair distribution, genitalia, and ability to respond sexually (both giving and receiving). Hartman and Fithian's (1974) idea of having individuals evaluate their physical being and the components from head to toe can be a valuable asset. Each spouse is asked to score him/herself on an imaginary continuum from 0 to 100, with 100 being maximum. Hartman and Fithian have found that those who like themselves give a rating of 85 to 100, and people with a poor self-concept ascribe themselves a rating of below 50.

Through completion of this sexual history, the therapist can identify sources of gross misinformation in the forms of myths, such as the importance of penis size, perceived "pathological" nature of group masturbation while in junior high, coitus is the only "right" way to achieve sexual satisfaction, the male is always the aggressor, and oral sex is "dirty," etc. In regard to the role of myths on the sexual performance of couples, Lederer and Jackson (1968, p. 123) have said: "If the various manifestations of sex were accepted as natural, and if people could abandon the view that there is a single absolute standard to be reached by all who are normal, the unhappiness of many couples would decrease and their performance would automatically improve."

The last area of concern in exploring the couple's sexual relationship revolves about their ability to communicate directly and honestly about their sexual likes and dislikes. It is not uncommon for the alcoholic, sexually dysfunctional couple to manifest marked inability to discuss their difficulty without hostility or other emotions that confuse and compound their dilemma.

Rather than attempting to give an overview of treatment techniques, it seems more appropriate to refer the reader to books such as Kaplan's *New Sex Therapy: Active Treatment of Sexual Dysfunction* (1974); Masters and Johnson's, *Human Sexual Inadequacy* (1970); and Hartman and Fithian's, *Treatment of Sexual Dysfunction: A Bio-Psycho-Social Approach* (1974). In these books and others like them, specific sexual techniques are presented in detail and accompanied in many cases with illustrations. The reader who refers to these resources will probably be struck by how relatively simplistic the techniques appear to be. Considering this, it must be remembered that (with the aid of these techniques) sex therapists are reporting success of up to 100 percent in treating some of the sexual dysfunctions explained earlier.

SUMMARY

The intent of this chapter was to present a discussion of the sexual component of the alcoholic's life. Attention was devoted to the alcoholic's sense of alienation, guilt, shame, anger, and reduced self-esteem as both a causative agent of sexual dysfunction and the consequence of involvement with alcohol. The vicious cycle of perceiving self as a sexual failure, and drinking to numb this sense of failure, is an often observed one in working with abusers. Attention was also devoted to the factors, specific to both males and females, which affect the development of sexual dysfunctions in alcoholics. A section was offered discussing what, in the author's opinion, are important considerations regarding how to talk about sexual matters in a facilitative fashion.

The chapter closed with a discussion of specific sexual dysfunctions and their treatment. Hopefully the reader developed an appreciation of the intricate role of sexuality in the treatment of alcoholism. Just as the alcoholism can be destructive to sex and marriage, so too can the schismatic marriage promote the alcoholism and sexual dysfunction development. As Hanson and Estes have stated: "Whether alcoholism is a result of sexual disturbance and marital dissatisfaction or a precursor of the marital dissonance is not presently well understood. It does seem clear, however, that overwhelming obstructions to creative and fulfilling sexual interaction, as experienced by many alcoholic men and women, can contribute to deterioration in the marital bonds" (1977, p. 71).

Chapter 8

MARITAL GROUP THERAPY

INTRODUCTION

ONE of the more prominently observed modalities of treatment used to address alcoholism today is group therapy. While groups are widely employed, marital groups are less frequent in their appearance. Considering the value and efficacy of marital group therapy it seems unfortunate to have to make this last statement. Many prominent clinicians and researchers, among them Satir (1964) and Lewis, Beavers, Gossett and Phillips (1976), have identified the marital dyad as a significant unit for intervention. Satir highlights this belief by referring to the parents as "the architects of the family." Acknowledging the centrality of the marital/parental dyad in the workings of any family, it seems to follow that marital group therapy would be utilized frequently in the process of helping the individual and family in the process of rehabilitation.

Smith and Alexander have offered the following regarding their experience in working with marital groups:

> In our counseling with couples in groups we find that when a group of couples, all experiencing troubled relationships, meet with competent therapists, there appears to be a sense of camaraderie and sharing in which there is a desire to aid others, as well as to work on solving the problems of their own relationship. There is a commitment to work together for change, not only for themselves but for the group as a whole. It also appears that the advantage of sharing similar experiences with other couples tends to increase the likelihood of achieving success in improving a couples relationship (1974, p. 3).

Certainly the above quote offers a sound rationale, but another clinician has provided an observation that this author believes

128

strengthens that offered by Smith and Alexander's: "In essence, a married couples group tends to operate as a 'third family' which in the last analysis means that it gives each individual and couple another chance to come to life and grow, whereas the real family (primary or present) has had a growth-thwarting effect" (Leichter, 1974, p. 142).

As the reader attends to the next section, the author is hopeful of clarifying the value of a marital group therapy approach by specifying what can be accomplished through utilization of this modality. The reader should also keep in mind the more obvious advantages of working within a group context such as: (1) *universality*—the couples realize the commonality of their difficulties and thus avoid the sense of shame and guilt arising from their continuing to believe they are "all alone"; (2) *economical*— if the therapist is working with ten to sixteen people it is certainly more cost effective than seeing only one or two people in that same time frame; (3) *satisfaction*—all of the participants have the opportunity to enhance their sense of self-esteem from becoming cognizant of the fact that by involving themselves they are also helping others; (4) *educational*—all can learn from one another how they have handled problems of a similar nature, and often people find it easier to see how others have achieved change as opposed to how they might be able to; and (5) *reality rub*—the group offers "many mirrors" for the individual couples to observe themselves and this is often much more effective than a couple receiving feedback from a counselor.

GOALS OF MARITAL GROUP THERAPY

The following are offered as examples of more prominent goals or purposes of marital group therapy with couples where one or both are alcoholic. The author is fully cognizant of the fact that each group leader will have a preferred mode of operating and thus may emphasize some of the following to the exclusion of others. In doing so the author believes effectiveness can still be present, but believes it is appropriate to be more exhaustive in this presentation in order to provide a "menu" of sorts from which group leaders might select and then direct their marital groups.

Sobriety

The author believes a continual effort must be made regarding the prominent place of sobriety in achieving a changed individual, marital and family life-style. It is unlikely that any change of significance will be achieved if the alcoholic drinking is continued. While acknowledgment regarding continued drinking remains with the individual, the author believes that the group leader should express the value of sobriety in the group whenever appropriate, and the opportunity is generally, freely available. Questions such as the following can be helpful in punctuating the prominence of the value of sobriety: "That sounds rough. How did you make it through that without drinking?" "How could that have been different for you without the drinking?" "You sound as though you're a completely different person sober. What advantages are there in sobriety for you as an individual as well as spouse and parent?" "How are you two closer in sobriety as opposed to when you were drinking?" While the Rand Report has stimulated the debate about the ability of the alcoholic to return to controlled drinking, the author believes sobriety should be the ultimate goal of treatment. There is sufficient evidence available that now suggests that at least some alcoholics have a genetic predisposition for alcoholism, which makes returning to alcohol much akin to a game of Russian roulette.

Enjoyment of Life While Sober

Helping the couple to develop sources of joy and pleasure without alcohol can be a crucial goal of marital group therapy. This can be most often best accomplished in the group context as each couple is afforded the opportunity to learn from the others present. It is not uncommon to find that over the years of alcoholic drinking, the couples' creativity and zest for developing and maintaining pleasure has significantly waned. By listening to others, new opportunities and ideas are discovered as hope for pleasure in sobriety is sparked. The group leader may even determine value in making this area the focus of at least one group meeting, as opposed to highlighting this dimension as it appears appropriate to the content being discussed. The author believes either of these approaches is good and has perceived equal success with both approaches.

Socialization

Alcoholics have often been referred to as a lonely and isolated group and most frequently so are their spouses. Certainly this can confound their other difficulties. Cadogan has said: "Social isolation, through an emotional incubation process, seems to increase alcoholics' fear of others and further reduces their ability to function socially. For some couples the marital group fills the social void in their lives" (1979, pp. 191-192). The group can serve as the "incubation place" for undeveloped and/or forgotten social skills that are not reliant upon alcoholic drinking. While this is occurring it is important for the group leader to be cognizant of the members becoming so attached to the group that they do not go outside of the immediate group to utilize their newly discovered social skills. For this reason, contacts outside of group social contacts should be reinforced and at times assigned as a task between group sessions. For instance, it helps at times to make assignments such as the following with the idea that each couple provides a report at the next session: invite a neighbor couple in for the evening or identify a couple you have not socialized with for some time, but would like to spend time with, and get together with them. Most often these assignments are completed and result in surprisingly satisfying experiences for the couples involved. While they, as a couple, may have been thinking of this for some time, they needed just the nudge that the assignment provided for them. Perhaps the quote from Forrest best summarizes the value of the group to the recovering alcoholic:

> People who have had little experience with alcohol-addicted individuals often fail to appreciate the profound significance of a group of alcoholics simply gettting together and relating on a sober basis. It is my feeling that any form of social interaction of a group nature which is non-drinking-oriented is extremely beneficial to the alcoholic's process of learning not to drink . . . . The group-oriented social nature of Alcoholics Anonymous is, in all probability, as much a part of this organization's success as any of the other aspects of the organization (Forrest, 1978, pp. 100-101).

While this statement is directed to the alcoholic, the author believes that it is also most often true of the nonalcoholic spouse as well. Just as they are learning now to relate more effectively to those outside of their own marital relationship, there is bound to be a spillover effect unto their own marital relationship, and vice versa, as greater interpersonal comfort is achieved.

Reduction of Interactional Anxiety

Directly related to socialization is interactional anxiety and its reduction in order to facilitate productive socialization. Cadogan has said: "Underlying the gregarious facade of many alcoholics is often a deep-seated and feared introversiveness. Their self-esteem is easily threatened and results in feelings of hostility that often leaves them tense and anxious in social situations" (Cadogan, 1979, p. 191). The type of anxiety identified here has often been attached to the etiology of alcoholism as the individual is rewarded for drinking through the numbing of the uncomfortable anxiety otherwise experienced. As this is considered, it becomes quite apparent that in order to diminish the attractiveness of alcohol, there is value in working at the reduction and/or elimination of these anxieties. Within the sanctuary afforded by the group, the participants can work towards this goal. The support experienced and learnings acquired via the group feedback process, and other interactions, typically prove invaluable in enhancing self-esteem and reducing unreasonable and often irrational fears and behaviors that have maintained the interactional anxiety.

Support

The process of recovery for the couple is in a very real way a time of transition. They are moving into new ways of thinking and behaving and for that very reason are probably somewhat uneasy. The familiar, regardless of how uncomfortable or counterproductive, provides a sense of security. As a new future is being created, support can be valuable, if not essential. Forrest has said: "Being able to share experiences which have often been most threatening, often antisocial, and perhaps even bizarre with others who have a personal history which includes these same behaviors and feelings enables the alcoholic (and nonalcoholic spouse) to perceive himself as something other than a social outcast and deviant" (Forrest, 1978, p. 98). This sharing, and awareness of being understood, can be among the most powerful of the various types of support a person can receive. This is the phenomena that Yalom (1970) has referred to as the "principle of universality." This "welcome to the human race" experience can serve as a powerful source of hope and motivation for the couples involved. Cadogan has stated the following as he discussed this phenomena:

> Alcoholics Anonymous has long know this and facilitates the experience by encouraging its members to openly discuss in the group their problems with alcohol. This discovery appears to help many alcoholics realize that their difficulties are less the result of being defective than of being human. This helps them to believe that their problems can be mastered or at least coped with. It also appears to enhance feelings of self-esteem when alcoholics know that their spouses are coming to similar realizations (Cadogan, 1979, p. 196).

Hope

The sense of universality is one powerful source of hope for the couples in a group. As the experience occurs, it facilitates the couple making a commitment to the group and the recovery/rehabilitation process. As Gwinner has said: "Perhaps the crucial ingredient in treatment success is not really treatment at all but rather the person's decision to seek treatment and to remain in treatment" (Gwinner, 1979, p. 118). Whether or not it is the "key ingredient," the decision to stay in treatment is significant, and the author believes this commitment is enhanced with the development of a sense of hope. This also underlines one of the values of having couples in various stages of recovery/rehabilitation in the group. Those couples who have made fairly significant and positive progress can serve as a source of hope for those in the earlier stages, just as those in the earlier stages serve to remind the more experienced couples of the advances they have made. This kind of beneficial reciprocity serves to accentuate another value of a marital group approach.

Insight and Education

The development of insight and educational matters are naturally a pervasive dimension of a marital group approach. Blume has said: "Successful adjustment to life without alcohol requires new responses to situations that would have prompted drinking in the past" (Blume, 1978, p. 70). As the couple endeavors to become different, there is significant value in their developing an understanding of how they have been and what they can do differently in order to achieve productive change. This may take the form of enhancing communication and/or parenting skills, improving their sexual relationship, developing new and more adaptive socialization skills, learning job-seeking skills, and many other topical areas. The group not only allows them the opportunity for learning from other's (spectator therapy) presentations of their progresses, but also by receiving feedback from other group members regarding how they and their plans and ideas are perceived.

Project CALM, at the Alcoholism Treatment Unit of the Brockton, Massachusetts Veterans Administration Medical Center, is an example of a marital group approach that emphasizes education. The director of this program, Timothy O'Farrell, is concerned with helping the couples in the group learn ways of preventing themselves from returning to old habits and becoming better able to cope should a relapse occur. The group approach is behavioral in nature with structured assignments for the couples. O'Farrell has described a core component of this program by saying: "Behavioral approaches to marriage therapy for the alcoholic stress specific techniques counselors can use to help couples learn new ways of behaving and communicating. These are practiced in the groups and assigned for use at home between sessions" (*NIAAA/ IFS*, 1979, p. 2). Preliminary studies have documented the success of this approach in helping couples to learn more effective ways of dealing with one another and their circumstances. Just as Project CALM stresses marital relationship building skills, the marital group therapist could choose to focus on sexual functioning, parenting, or any other focus areas. It is not uncommon to find special interest groups "spinning off" from a more generally focused group as specific areas are worked with. If there are not enough interested in a specific area to justify developing a subgroup, this is an area that could certainly be worked with more exhaustively in separate sessions with the concerned couple. As Masters and Johnson (1970) have indicated, so many sexual problems stem from a lack of information and knowledge, so too do many other human problems that confront the recovering alcoholic and spouse. For this reason the educational value of a group experience should not be minimized and regarded as elementary or not "really therapy."

Problem Solving

This is an area that can often comprise an element where education for the couple is particularly urgent. As indicated elsewhere in this book, alcoholics and their spouses so often come from disruptive, chaotic families where appropriate problem solving was never modeled for them. More typically their problem-solving skills are more reactive in nature and often do nothing other than confound their problems. While some members may push for answers or solutions to their problems, it is generally more valuable to focus on the problem-solving process. As Cadogan has said: "It should be stressed that discovering the processes involved in problem solving is a more important part of the marital group's work than finding the solutions themselves. The group's emphasis on the process of problem solving rather than the problems themselves, allows for greater generalization on the part of its members" (Cadogan, 1979, p. 188). While couples may get ideas regarding solutions to their problems from listening to others, the more crucial concern is with their learning more appropriate problem-solving skills. The process of defining a problem, discovering options and alternatives, evaluating alternatives, implementing and evaluating effectiveness are the components of effective problem solving and are important to be learned. Certainly effective communication is a key variable in this process for the couple, and communication skills and effective problem solving can often be woven together efficiently. A couples group of this nature is generally conducive to this type of effort because so many of the problems and concerns identified are cogent to all involved. This commonality of problems, and the inappropriate means of problem solving, seem to be one of the other variables that lends itself to the development and maintenance of group cohesiveness. This author's experience has documented the manner in which couples come to appreciate the complex and interconnected nature of their difficulties so that they discard the notion that all that is needed for a new life is sobriety. The dispelling of this myth of sobriety as a panacea is an important step in their movement toward more productive living.

Communication

"Communication, verbal or nonverbal, is the vehicle through which family members touch each other and regulate their emotional closeness or distance. Every interaction between two or more family members involves not only the sharing of information, but also the shaping and determining of the relationship involved" (Barnard and Corrales, 1979, p. 172).

This process of managing social distance, exchanging information, and shaping relationships can be readily observed in the process of the marital group. Regardless of the format or content of the group, communication is occurring and is readily available for the therapeutic endeavor. As has been said before, "communication is the one thing man cannot not do." Considering this, the facilitator has a literal "therapeutic gold mine" available for facilitating change in the relationships represented. As mentioned in Chapter 2, the facilitator has many variables that can be worked with under the umbrella of communication.

The person facilitating the group may choose to work with the communication dimension as the opportunity affords itself or may choose to address the area by introducing a more formal program such as the Minnesota Couples Communication Program (Miller, Nunnally, and Wackman, 1979). This program focusses on levels of communication, styles, or ways in which people communicate; basic components of the human experience that are vital to effective communication; and specific skills that enhance couple communication. The decision regarding how to deal with enhancement of communication in the context of the group must be made by the facilitator. Oftentimes this will be identified as a specific request from the group members and thus group time can be appropriated for this area. While the author has conducted groups using both of these approaches (group structured as communication oriented, and group more unstructured with time devoted to communication enhancement as appropriate), it seems that in general, communication enhancement can be easily woven into the fabric of the ongoing group, and done so in this fashion most effectively.

As someone speaks for themselves and makes a distinctive and complete "I" message, this can be acknowledged and reinforced immediately. The behavioral psychologists have demonstrated that immediate reinforcement is most valuable and that the likelihood of skills generalizing to others is most likely to occur when behaviors under consideration can be reinforced by an authority figure in the presence of those who will ideally model the reinforced behaviors. As the facilitator reinforces the individual who sent a clear "I" message, the likelihood of group members modeling this behavior is increased. For purposes of this example, "I" messages were used. It could have just as easily been the process of someone who utilizes other effective skills such as checking out or making sure what they thought they heard is what the sender intended to say, or the sender who provides behavioral documentation of behaviors that have resulted in the beliefs he(she) has formulated, or the individual who in spite of being hurt formulates and sends a congruent message that is clear and concise on all levels.

It is also a tremendous advantage of marital groups to have the various participants practice newly acquired communication skills with persons other than their spouses in the group setting. The histories of the couples, where one or both are recovering alcoholics, result in a tremendous carryover of affect that may prove to be debilitating in acquiring the skills necessary to their resolving issues. As they practice they can develop a greater comfort level with the new skills and then transfer them to the marital relationship.

Certainly the area of interpersonal communication and skill enhancement is crucial to most of the marriages. Forrest has said:

> Involvement in the marital couples' group enables both patient and spouse the opportunity to begin to communicate and relate to one another more effectively. The alcoholic marriage appears to be predicated on both a lack of interpersonal communication as well as distorted or essentially parataxic patterns of communication. It is not at all surprising to find couples who have lived together for as long as twenty years in the absence of effective relating and communicating . . . . Disclosing, sharing, dealing with more effective decision making are but a few sources of gain (Forrest, 1978, p. 108).

So often these marriages have firmly entrenched communication patterns, which are out of the couples awareness, and yet keep them ensnarled in their counterproductive ways. The wife who blames extensively and the husband who relies upon being always reasonable and explaining his behavior can be used as an example. The more the wife blames the more he explains. The more he explains the more she believes he must be "blame worthy." The more he feels blamed the more he experiences a need to provide her with "corrective" information, which does nothing more than intensify and calcify their interaction. Both are assuming and, on the basis of their improper assumptions, engaging in communication behavior that does not correct the assumptions but, rather, strengthens them. In this regard, the author has found it valuable to introduce the couples to the styles of communication as presented by Satir (1972).

Satir discusses four prominent styles of communication used by people to manipulate and be dishonest with one another. The four styles identified are the placater, the blamer, the computer, and the distracter. The placating style is used to prevent others from becoming angry. The person using this style talks in an ingratiating way, trying to please. This person talks as though they are helpless and totally at the mercy of others. The blaming style, as you might guess, results in faults being found, dictating, and bossing others around. Those around this person vacillate between feeling humiliated, angry, defensive, and defeated. The computing style is manifested in very reasonable, very correct, aloof communication with little if any feeling demonstrated. Those around this type of communication become bored, irritated and often defensive. The distracter, or person manifesting the distracting style, sends messages that are irrelevant to what those around are communicating. A response is seldom if ever to the point. Those around this individual often find themselves frustrated and angry. While these four styles are dramatic, most of us use all of them to one degree or another, and most often they are not productive to our relationships.

These styles can be introduced to the group and then have them "try on" the behaviors in order to determine which styles seem to "fit" them. They are encouraged to develop a sensitivity to each of the four styles and identify which they believe are used most frequently. Once they have identified the one or two styles believed to be relied upon most often, they can then negotiate a contract with their spouses designed to effect change. An example might be the following: the wife identifies herself as a blamer and the husband himself as a placater. During the ensuing week between group sessions they agree to keep "score" or a record of

how often they each catch themselves utilizing their self-diag-
nosed, dominant style. Their records are then brought back into
the next group session and the experience is discussed. This can
be continued from week to week in order to determine the
progress they make in diminishing the old, more destructive
behaviors and replacing them with more facilitative skills and
behaviors.

An exercise can be introduced to help the participants diagnose
themselves as well as emphasize the futility of attempting to
develop a relationship utilizing these communication styles.
After introducing the four styles just described, the group is
divided into small groups of three or four. Each person is
assigned a particular communication style and instructed to send
messages portraying only that style. Each small group is then
instructed to imagine themselves as a set of people who have not
seen one another for some years, and they are to decide how they
might best spend the next few days together. They discuss this for
three minutes. While this task will result in chaos (and probably
many laughs), it accentuates what all of them are so familiar
with. Upon completion of the first three minutes they switch
roles and continue. At the end of this experience each is asked to
identify which of the four communication styles best illustrates
their behavior in relation to their spouse. Generally a lively
discussion follows and results in the contracting of new behavior
for the time between this session and the next.

This is one example of several different types of exercises that
can be used to help the couples better understand their communication patterns and begin to develop more effective ways of
relating. There are many examples of other exercises contained in
publications such as those by Miller, Nunnally, and Wackman
(1976, 1979).

One vital component of human behavior that often confounds
communication in an alcoholic population is that of feelings.
Blume has indicated that alcoholics drink for many reasons, but
two that present significant difficulties for the recovering alcoholic are as follows:

> The first of these is drinking to relieve painful feeling states. When
> drinking, the alcoholic may even consume alcohol in anticipation of
> such feelings. Thus various emotional states come to be perceived as the
> state of needing a drink and are poorly recognized or sorted out from

another. In the process of living without this drug, it becomes important for the alcoholic to identify and label his emotional states in order to make an adequate response to his distress. Positive feelings may also be poorly identified by the drinking alcoholic, who perceives them as the urge for a drink to celebrate or confuses them with his drug induced euphoria. These positive feelings are the building blocks of self-esteem during recovery. Recognition and identification of feeling states thus becomes a major component of therapy (Blume. 1978, p. 70).

Just as the adequate identification and expression of feelings are crucial to the enhancement of the individual alcoholic, so to are they to the betterment of the marriage. The couple probably has a history of volatile and inappropriate expression of feelings that has resulted in them being over-controlling and/or outright denial of their feelings. This process of attempting to hold their feelings in check is what often accounts for the confusing double messages so frequently observed in these marriages. While the spouse uses words to communicate one message and feeling state, their nonverbal behavior may communicate a contradictory message and feeling state. Regardless of which of the messages the receiver responds to, the response will only be partial and thus potentially frustrating and confounding to the overall relationship. As a result, as with the individual alcoholic, the spouses can benefit from learning how to identify and acknowledge each of the various feelings they are experiencing and then communicate them directly and with the proper acknowledgment they are due. Until the couple can improve the clear communication of their feelings, it is unlikely that much progress will be made.

Overcoming Denial

Denial is a phenomena that receives much attention in the treatment of alcoholism. It also is frequently observed in marital groups. Denial is prominent with alcoholics as they deny the severity of their condition and need for significant change. So often it is observed that without a crisis the alcoholic is able to maintain the denial system. Another form of denial that is often observed in the marital dyad consists of denying the presence of problems other than the drinking. Assuming action is being taken to correct the drinking situation, the couple can continue to deceive themselves by believing that cessation of the drinking is the panacea. Both spouses must acknowledge any other difficulties in their relationship that are in need of their attention.

The group process can be invaluable in helping a couple confront and examine their own denial. Not only can the material being denied be confronted, but the couple can also learn from the other couples that their problems are not that unique and that many others have already successfully wrestled with them. The couple who is denying the sexual area of their relationship can acquire courage to confront this area as they observe other couples successfully handling the sexual component. Or this same couple may, in the course of their interaction, give another couple in the group a cue suggestive of their denied sexual problems. The second couple has already struggled with the same issue and is thus sensitive to the signs contained in the behavior of the first couple. At this point the second couple can engage the other couple as a resource and source of support and guidance regarding how they have sought to resolve their sexual difficulties. This kind of "cross encounter" within the group is one of the distinguishing strengths of this modality, particularly in regards to dealing with denial. With the aid of the facilitator, the confrontation of the denial can be readily defined as concern for those whose denial is being questioned.

Reduce Family Pathology

"The pathological traits of some alcoholics are complemented or neutralized by the pathological traits of their spouse. Improvement in one partner's disorder could have a deleterious effect on the relationship in that the pathological needs of the other partner would no longer be satisfied by the relationship" (Cadogan, 1979, p. 194). These ideas of Cadogan summarize well one of the often observed manifestations of pathology observed in the couples involved in the group. Along with the more blatant forms of pathology, which may surface as the couple adjusts to sobriety, there is the prominence of immaturity that is demonstrated. Immaturity is observed in the form of destructive competitiveness, inability to adaptively communicate feelings and intentions, self-pity and martydom, and inability to manifest empathy for one another. Most frequently the other group members are quick to observe and acknowledge this in others as a result of the likelihood of them experiencing and/or demonstrating these same behaviors in the past. Many who have facilitated these groups have commented on how quickly participants can identify these behaviors in others while they may appear blind to their own possession of the same idiosyncrasies. This type of cross encounter is what provides the group not only vitality, but it's therapeutic value for those involved.

Along with the pathology central to the marital relationship, the pathology present between the parental and child subsystems is also often encountered. The difficulties between the couples in the group and their children is crucial here, along with difficulties between the couples and their parents. The process of clarifying and legitimatizing relationships with the generation ahead and behind these couples often becomes a focus of concern for the group. Just as there may have been physical, sexual, and emotional abuse between these parents and their children, it is frequently observed that many of the same phenomena occurred between these couples and their parents. Even if there is not apparent potential for resolution between these couples and their parents, the goal becomes that of helping them to change and more adequately resolve their perceptions and reactions to the past. It is often advantageous to help the couples realize that they have a choice in relation to the past. They can use the past to clutter and contaminate the present and future or use it to learn from, and enlighten and improve, their present and future. While none of us can change our past, we all have the potential of responding to and utilizing the past in either of these two ways.

The group often proves itself to be most valuable in helping the individuals and couples in making more productive use of the past. The various couples soon learn about the principle of universality in the groups in the form of recognizing the similarities of their experiences with children and parents. Once this universality is acknowledged, the group members seem to become enthusiastic with regards to learning from one another how they have changed behaviors and perceptions in a fashion that has been most productive.

ISSUES TO CONSIDER FOR THE LEADER

Every group leader has a number of issues that need to be

considered and hopefully resolved prior to the group starting. While it is always valuable to maintain the potential for flexibility in working with this population, there is an equally strong need for order and parameters within which the group can function. The group leader arriving at decisions with regards to issues such as those about to be identified can go a long way in providing the group with the order and sense of stability that seems so typical of the more successful groups.

Pre-Group Interview

Many have identified the value of a pre-group interview (Bates and Johnson, 1972; and Corey and Corey, 1977). This pre-group interview allows the leader the opportunity to determine the goals of the couple and the likelihood of the group experience being of value to them. It may be determined that the couple is too disturbed to benefit from the group. Couples who are obviously more disturbed than others can end up either monopolizing the group or terminating quickly as they realize others are considerably more functional than themselves. Neither of these possibilities is a productive outcome of the group.

The interview prior to the group, while time consuming, also has the value of allowing the leaders to communicate to the couples their intentions for the group and means they intend to utilize in order to facilitate the experience. This is not only an ethical practice, but can save all concerned much frustration at a later point in the group's life. The leaders can also develop contracts with the couple's (based upon the couple's established goals) that can then be used by the leaders in a post-group interview to assess the effectiveness of the experience.

Closed vs. Open Format

A closed group infers that no new members are added after the group is commenced. Of course, an open group indicates the potential is there for members to be added as the group progresses. A closed group seems to facilitate the development of intimacy and cohesion, but this is offset by the stimulation that new members can provide in the open group format. Regardless of which format is adopted, this issue should be resolved prior to the group beginning so that everyone has the same understanding.

The author has found that the closed group format is most therapeutically intense. The cohesion, intimacy, and trust, which are facilitated in the closed group format, seem crucial to a more intense therapeutic effort. If the group is going to be more educational and/or problem solving in orientation, an open group format seems appropriate and stimulating to the process.

Confidentiality

This is an issue that should be addressed in the pre-group interview and at various phases of the group's development. The leaders should identify ways in which they may be expected, or required (court ordered), to share information acquired from the group process. If this is not clarified, and group members learn at a later date about the leader discussing material from the group outside of the group's parameter, it is likely going to be a difficult task at best for the leader to regain the group's trust.

The group leaders should emphasize that they cannot insure that all members will maintain confidences. While this may result in some members being hesitant to involve themselves fully, it is the most ethically sound position for the leader to assume. This is a particularly sensitive issue, as many who have worked with alcoholics have identified them as being suspicious of others anyway.

The author believes that penalties for violation of confidentiality in the group should be predetermined and communicated to all at the outset of the group. Termination of the privilege of continuing in the group is the penalty most often identified.

Ground Rules

One essential ground rule, or guideline, for group participation is that of confidentiality. Beyond maintaining confidences, the leaders need to decide about rules for other behaviors. It is always advisable to identify these guidelines prior to beginning a group in order to prevent having to make rules as crises are met and thus conveying a disorganized or punitive image to the members.

Examples of areas around which it is advisable to have gound rules established are lateness; absences; attending meetings under the influence of alcohol and other drugs; smoking or not;

grounds for termination of membership; responsibilities of leader and members; cliques developing and discussing group activities outside of the group and thus dissipating energy; what is "off limits" for group consideration and processing without both spouses agreeing; and, where appropriate, expectations regarding assignments given by the leader.

Size

Certainly the success and progress of a group is dependent to some degree upon the size of a group. In the large group (more than twelve members), rapport and trust are developed more slowly. The large group also has a greater likelihood of having couples get "lost in it." Simultaneously, a small group may not allow the couples enough of a sense of anonymity or safety in being able to retreat for the time being.

This author concurs with Smith and Alexander (1974) and Corey and Corey (1977) in believing that a couples group comprised of about twelve members is an optimum number for maximum effectiveness. This number allows the leader to be alert to all present and yet large enough to provide facilitative stimulation in the form of a variety of perceptions and experiences. While all in a group this size feel the opportunity to contribute, they also are provided enough of an opportunity to withdraw from active participation periodically and engage in spectator therapy (receiving therapeutic benefit from observing others).

Temporal Limits

The author believes that temporal limits are most appropriately set in accordance with the purpose of the group and size. If the group is educational and problem specific in nature, a relatively short time frame may be appropriate. An example of this type may be the group that is designed to provide education and training in the area of communication. For this purpose a set of four weekly sessions of two hours may be sufficient. A parent education group may address its goals in six meetings spaced a week apart. For a group of twelve or so members, which is geared to focus on the marital and family relationships, the author believes a contract of three to six months is most appropriate.

Forrest (1978) has indicated that he believes a group of six months in duration is important for the alcoholic attempting to establish long-term sobriety. This author believes a similar period of time is important for the relationship that is attempting to adapt to sobriety and make changes, which can also enhance their relationship. Regardless of whatever the temporal parameter selected, it is helpful to identify a specific termination point. This can be a great aid in preventing dawdling and malingering by the couples involved. At the end of the contracted period of time, the leader can afford the opportunity for further group or individual experience as it seems appropriate.

Physical Considerations

While this is rather obvious as a concern, the author has heard of groups that were a "bust" as a result of improper consideration being given to the physical environment. The leader must insure that adequate space is available to accommodate the number involved and various exercises that may be employed with the group. The alcoholic population seems notorious for their smoking and, assuming that smoking is allowed, consideration should be given to ventilation. Thought should also be given to lighting and furniture that seems most appropriate for the purpose of the group.

Evaluation

Evaluation of the group experience is valuable for all concerned. The leaders can assess their approach and techniques, and the participants are afforded the opportunity of reflecting on their experience in a structured fashion, which can often facilitate the integration of learnings. While evaluation is typically thought of as occurring at the end of an experience, the author also believes there is value in evaluating group progress midway in the life of the group as well. This can be done informally by simply setting time aside to solicit corrective feedback and can be utilized to adjust the group process to more appropriately meet the needs of the participants. The author has known of some leaders who do this routinely at the end of each session with reportedly positive results.

Terminal evaluation may take the form of collecting data from objective tests administered on a pre-group basis as well and/or assess the degree to which goals established in the pre-group interview were met. Corey and Corey identify a number of questions that can be useful for evaluation, such as: "What general effect, if any, has your group experience had on your life? What were the highlights of the group experience for you? What perceptions of the group leaders and their styles do you have? Did the group experience have any negative effects upon you? What effects do you think your participation in the group had on the significant people in your life? If a close friend were to ask you today to tell in a sentence or two what the group meant to you, how would you respond?" (1977, pp. 116-117). Certainly the reader might have particular questions to pose to the participants that would be even more valuable than these, but the author believes they are good examples of types of queries to present.

MULTIPLE FAMILY GROUP THERAPY

As this chapter has focussed on marital group therapy, as applied to alcoholism, the author would feel negligent in closing without mentioning Multiple Family Group Therapy (MFGT). This approach is very similar in design and purpose to marital group therapy. The primary difference being that of including entire families in the group rather than just the marital dyad. Laqueur, the individual primarily responsible for the most creditable writings on this approach, has summarized what MFGT is, by stating: "Multiple family therapy is a tool to teach individual families a great deal about their behavior by setting up mirrors (in reality and subsequently on film and on videotape) in which they can compare the things they are doing to each other" (1972, p. 633).

For the reader interested in further exploring this approach, the following articles are recommended: Laqueur, 1972a, 1972b, 1976; and Laqueur, LaGurt, and Morong, 1971. Through utilization of this approach the issue of total family pathology is addressed more directly than through utilization of marital group therapy alone.

SUMMARY

Marital group therapy, as one variant of family therapy, is a mode of treatment that has demonstrated itself to be a valuable tool in the treatment of alcoholism and the related relationship issues. This chapter was designed to discuss this approach as it applies to the treatment of the alcoholic in this context.

After an introduction to marital group therapy in the field of alcoholism treatment, the author turned his attention to the goals of this approach. The following were presented and discussed in this section: sobriety; enjoyment of life while sober; socialization; reduction of interactional anxiety; support; hope; insight and education; problem solving; communication; overcoming denial; and, the reduction of family pathology. Various practical ideas regarding implementation within these particular goals were also discussed.

From goals of marital group therapy, the chapter was directed to the issues that seem important for the group leader to consider. Issues discussed were: pre-group interview; closed vs. open format; confidentiality; ground rules; size; temporal limits; physical considerations; and finally evaluation. The chapter was closed with a brief overview of multiple family group therapy as a treatment modality and is closely related to marital group therapy.

BIBLIOGRAPHY

Al-Anon Family Group Headquarters. *The Dilemma of the Alcoholic Marriage*, P.O. Box 182, Madison Square Station, New York, 1971.

Andolfi, M. *Family Therapy: An Interactional Approach*. New York: Plenum Press, 1979.

Bailey, M.B.: *Alcoholism and Family Casework*. New York: Community Council of Greater New York, 1968.

Bandler, R., Grinder, J., and Satir, V.: *Changing With Families*. Palo Alto: Science and Behavior Books, 1976.

Bandler, R., and Grinder, J.: *The Structure of Magic*. Palo Alto: Science and Behavior Books, 1975.

Bandler, R., and Grinder, J.: *Patterns of the Hypnotic Techniques of Milton H. Erickson, M.D.*, Vol. I. Cupertino, California: Meta Publications, 1975.

Barnard, Charles P., and Corrales, Ramon G.: *The Theory and Technique of Family Therapy*. Springfield, Illinois: Thomas, 1979.

Bates, M.M., and Johnson, D.C.: *Group Leadership*. Denver: Love Publishing, 1972.

Beckman, L.J.: Reported effects of alcohol on the sexual feelings and behavior of women alcoholics and nonalcoholics. *Journal of Studies on Alcohol, 40:* 272-281, 1979.

Belliveau, F., and Richter, L.: *Understanding Human Sexual Inadequacy*. Boston: Little, Brown and Co., 1970.

Berenson, D.: Alcohol and the family system. In Guerin, P. (Ed.): *Family Therapy and Practice*. New York: Gardner Press, 1976.

Berg, B., and Roseblum, N.: Fathers in family therapy: A survey of family therapists. *Journal of Marriage and Family Counseling, 3:*85-91, 1977.

Bertalanffy, L. Von: General system theory and psychiatry. In Arieti, S. (Ed.): *American Handbook of Psychiatry*. New York: Basic Books, 1966.

Bing, E.: The conjoint family drawing. *Family Process, 9:*173-194, 1970.

Bloch, D.A.: The clinical home visit. In Bloch, Donald A. (Ed.): *Techniques of Family Therapy: A Primer*. New York: Grune and Stratton, 1973.

Blume, S.B.: Group psychotherapy in the treatment of alcoholism. In Zimber, S., Wallace, J., and Blume, S.B. (Eds.): *Practical Approaches to Alcoholism Psychotherapy*. New York: Plenum Press, 1978.

Boszormenyi-Nagy, I., and Spark, G.: *Invisible Loyalties*. New York: Medical

Division of Harper and Row, 1973.

Bowen, M.: Family systems approach to alcoholism. *Addictions, 21*(2):28-39, 1974.

Bowen, M.: Alcoholism as viewed through family systems theory and family psychotherapy. *Annals of the New York Academy of Science, 233:*115-122, 1974.

Byles, J.A.: Violence, alcohol problems and other problems in disintegrating families. *Journal of Studies on Alcohol, 39*(3):551-554, 1978.

Cadogan, D.A.: Marital group therapy in alcoholism treatment. In Kaufman, E., and Kaufmann, P. (Eds.): *Family Therapy of Drug and Alcohol Abuse.* New York: Gardner Press, 1979.

Chassel, J.: Family Constellation in the etiology of essential alcoholism. *Psychiatry, 1:*473-503, 1938.

Cohen, P.T.: A new approach to the treatment of male alcoholics and their families. *American Journal of Orthopsychiatry, 36:*247-248, 1966.

Coleman, S., and Davis, D.: Family therapy and drug abuse: A national survey. *Family Process, 17*(1):21-30, 1978.

Corey, G., and Corey, M.S.: *Groups: Process and Practice.* Monterey, California: Brooks/Cole Publishers, 1977.

Cork, R.M.: *The Forgotten Children.* Toronto: Alcoholism and Drug Addiction Research Foundation, 1969.

Davis, D.I.: Forum: Family therapy for the drug user: Conceptual and practical considerations. *Drug Forum, 6:*197-199, 1977-1978.

Davis, D., Berenson, D., Steinglass, P., and Davis, S.: The adaptive consequences of drinking. *Psychiatry, 37:*209-215, 1974.

DeBurger, J.E.: Sex in troubled marriages. In Gross, L. (Ed.): *Sexual Issues in Marriage.* Holliswood, New York: Spectrum Publications, 1975.

Dodson, L.S., and Kurpius, D.: *Family Counseling: A Systems Approach.* Muncie, Indiana: Accelerated Development Inc., 1977.

Doyle, E.L.: Female sexual conditioning. In Stahmann, R.F., and Hiebert, W.J. (Eds.): *Klemer's Counseling in Marital and Sexual Problems.* Baltimore: Williams and Wilkins Co., 1977.

Edwards, P., Harvey, C., and Whitehead, P.: Wives of alcoholics: A critical review and analysis. *Quarterly Journal of Studies on Alcohol, 34:*112-132, 1973.

Ellis, A.: Sex problems of couples seen for marriage counseling. In Ard, B., and Ard, C. (Eds.): *Handbook of Marriage Counseling.* Palo Alto: Science and Behavior Books, 1969.

Erikson, E.: *Childhood and Society.* New York: Grune and Stratton, 1950.

Forrest, G.G.: *The Diagnosis and Treatment of Alcoholism.* Springfield, Illinois: Thomas, 1978.

Fullmer, D.: Family group consultations. *Elementary School Guidance and Counseling, 7*(2):130-136, 1972.

Gamage, J.R.: *Management of Adolescent Drug Misuse: Clinical, Psychological and Legal Perspectives.* Beloit, Wisconsin: STASH Press, 1973.

Goodwin, D.W.: Is alcoholism hereditary: A review and critique. *Archives of General Psychiatry, 25:*545-549, 1971.

Goodwin, D.W., Schulsinger, F., Hermansen, L., Guze, S.B., and Winokur, G.: Alcohol problems in adoptees raised apart from alcoholic biologic parents. *Archives of General Psychiatry, 28*:238-243, 1973.

Grinder, J., and Bandler, R.: *The Structure of Magic.* Palo Alto: Science and Behavior Books, 1976, vol. II.

Grinder, J., Delozier, J., and Bandler, R.: *Patterns of the Hypnotic Techniques of Milton H. Erickson, M.D.* Cupertino, California: Meta Publications, 1977, vol. II.

Group for the Advancement of Psychiatry. *Assessment of Sexual Dysfunction.* New York: Jason Aronson, 1974.

Gwinner, P.: Treatment approaches. In Grant, M., and Gwinner, P. (Eds.): *Alcoholism in Perspective.* Baltimore: University Park Press, 1979.

Haley, J.: *Problem Solving Therapy.* San Francisco: Jossey-Bass Publishers, 1976.

Hanson, K.J., and Estes, N.J.: Dynamics of alcoholic families. In Estes, N., and Heinemann, M.E. (Eds.): *Alcoholism: Development, Consequences, and Interventions.* Saint Louis: The C.V. Mosby Company, 1977.

Hartman, W., and Fithian, M.: *Treatment of Sexual Dysfunctions: A Bio-Psycho-Social Approach.* Long Beach, California: Center for Marital and Sexual Studies, 1974.

Howard, D., and Howard, N.: Treatment of the significant other. In Zimberg, S. et al. (Eds.): *Practical Approaches to Alcoholism Psychotherapy.* New York: Plenum Press, 1978.

Irwin, E., and Mallory, E.: Family puppet interview. In Howells, J.G. (Ed.): *Advances in Family Psychiatry.* New York: International Universities Press, 1979.

Jackson, J.: The adjustment of the family to the crisis of alcoholism. *Quarterly Journal of Studies of Alcohol, 15*(4), 1954.

Jellinek, E.M.: *The Disease Concept of Alcoholism.* New Haven, Connecticut: College and University Press, 1960.

Johnson, V.E.: *I'll Quit Tomorrow.* New York: Harper and Row, 1973.

Kaplan, H.S. *The New Sex Therapy.* New York: Brunner/Mazel. 1974.

Kaufman, E., and Kaufmann, P.: Multiple family therapy: A new direction in the treatment of drug abuse. *American Journal of Drug and Alcohol Abuse, 4*(4):467-478, 1977.

Keller, J.: *Alcohol: A Family Affair,* Kroc Foundation, 1977.

Keller, M. (Ed.): Trends in treatment of alcoholism. *In Second Special Report to the U.S. Congress on Alcohol and Health.* Washington, D.C.: Department of Health, Education and Welfare, 1974, pp. 145-167.

Kephart, W.M.: Drinking and marital disruption: A research note. *Quarterly Journal of Studies on Alcohol, 15*:63-73, 1954.

Kissin, B.: Theory and practice in the treatment of alcoholism. In Kissin, B., and Begleiter, H. (Eds.): *Treatment and Rehabilitatoin of the Chronic Alcoholic: The Biology of Alcoholism.* New York: Plenum Press, 1977.

Knight, R.: The dynamics and treatment of chronic alcohol addiction. *Bulletin of the Menninger Clinic, 1*:233-250, 1937.

Kwiatkowska, H.: Family art therapy. *Family Process, 6*:37-55, 1967.

Laquer, H.P.: Mechanisms of change in multiple family therapy. In Sager, C., and Kaplan, H.S. (Eds.): *Progress in Group and Marital Family Therapy.* New York: Brunner/Mazel, 1972.

Laquer, H.P.: Multiple family therapy. In Ferber, A., Mendelsohn, M., and Napier, A. (Eds.): *The Book of Family Therapy.* New York: Science House, 1972.

Laquer, H.P.: Multiple family therapy. In Guerin, P.J. (Ed.): *Family Therapy: Theory and Practice.* New York, Gardner Press, 1976, pp. 405-416.

Laquer, H.P., LaGurt, A., and Morong, E.: Multiple family therapy: Further developments. In Haley, J. (Ed.): *Changing Families.* New York: Grune and Stratton, 1971.

Lederer, W., and Jackson, D.D.: *The Mirages of Marriage.* New York: W.W. Norton and Company, 1968.

Leichter, E.: Treatment of married couples groups. In Nichols, W. (Ed.): *Marriage and Family Therapy.* Minneapolis: National Council on Family Relations, 1974.

LeMere, F., and Smith, J.W.: Alcohol induced sexual impotence. *American Journal of Psychiatry, 130*:212-213, 1973.

Lewis, J.M.: *How's Your Family?* New York: Brunner/Mazel, 1979.

Lewis, J.M. et al.: *No Single Thread: Psychological Health in Family Systems.* New York: Brunner/Mazel, 1976.

LoPiccolo, J., and LoPiccolo, L.: *Handbook of Sex Therapy.* New York: Plenum Press, 1978.

Masters, W.H., and Johnson, V.E.: *Human Sexual Inadequacy.* Boston: Little, Brown and Company, 1970.

Masters, W.H., and Johnson, V.E.: *Human Sexual Response.* Boston: Little, Brown and Company, 1966.

Mayer, J., and Filstead, W.: The adolescent alcohol involvement scale. *Journal of Studies on Alcohol, 40*:291-300, 1979.

McPherson, S., Brackelmanns, W., and Newman, L.: Stages in the family therapy of adolescents. *Family Process, 13*:77-94, 1974.

Meeks, D.E.: Family therapy. In Tarter, R., and Sugarman, A. (Eds.): *Alcoholism: Interdisciplinary Approaches to an Enduring Problem.* New York: Addison/Wesley, 1976.

Meiselman, K.C.: *Incest.* San Francisco: Jossey/Bass Publishers, 1978.

Miller, S., Nunnally, E., and Wackman, D.: *Alive and Aware.* Minneapolis: Interpersonal Communication Programs, 1979.

Miller, S., Nunnally, E., and Wackman, D.: *Alive and Aware: Improving Communication in Relationships.* Minneapolis: Interpersonal Communication Programs, 1977.

Miller, S., Nunnally, E., and Wackman, D.: *Couple Workbook: Increasing Awareness and Communication Skills.* Minneapolis: Interpersonal Communication Programs, 1976.

Miller, S., Nunnally, E., and Wackman, D.: *Talking Together: Couples Communication I.* Minneapolis: Interpersonal Communication Programs, 1979.

Minuchin, S.: *Families and Family Therapy.* Cambridge, Massachusetts: Harvard University Press, 1974.

Minuchin, S. et al.: *Families of Slums.* New York: Basic Books, 1967

Minuchin, S., and Montalvo, B.: Techniques for working with disorganized low socio-economic families. *American Journal of Orthopsychiatry, 37*:880-887, 1967.

Napier, A., and Whitaker, C.: *The Family Crucible.* New York: Harper and Row, 1978.

NIAAA/IFS: New directions stresses family therapy approach. December 31, 1979, p. 5.

NIAAA/IFS: Califano cites need for continued research. November 30, 1978, p. 1.

NIAAA/IFS: Couples group therapy compared in VA study. November 28, 1979, p. 2.

NIAAA/IFS: Summary of third report on alcohol and health. November 30, 1978, pp. 3-7.

NIAAA/IFS: Therapists need sexuality knowledge. September 20, 1978, p. 5

NIAAA/IFS: Clinic aids children of alcoholic patients. March 3, 1978, p. 6.

NIAAA/IFS: Research reports extend knowledge of fetal alcohol syndrome effects. July 29, 1976, p. 4.

NIAAA/IFS: Family therapy approaches studies. April 12, 1976.

NIAAA/IFS: Family therapy is primary treatment for children and their alcoholic parents. January 7, 1976, p. 5.

NIAAA/IFS: Familization therapy treats relatives as co-patients. September 19, 1975, p. 3.

NIAAA/IFS: Family counseling enhances chances of early identification, treatment. April 26, 1975, p. 1.

NIAAA/IFS: Family therapy helpful, social workers say. April 1, 1975, p. 3.

NIAAA/IFS: Children of alcoholic parents need professional evaluation. October 10, 1975, p. 4.

NIAAA/IFS: Featured speakers at NCA meeting discuss TV drinking, alcoholism funds, family therapy. July 14, 1974, p. 4.

Paolino, T.J., and McCrady, B.S.: *The Alcoholic Marriage: Alternative Perspectives.* New York: Grune and Stratton, 1977.

Papp, P. et al.: Family sculpting in preventive work with well families. *Family Process, 12*:197-212, 1973.

Reddy, B.: *Alcoholism: A Family Illness.* Park Ridge, Illinois, Lutheran General Hospital, 1973.

Reed, D.M.: Male sexual conditioning. In Stahmann, R.F., and Heibert, W.J. (Eds.): *Klemer's Counseling in Marital and Sexual Problems.* Baltimore: Williams and Wilkins Company, 1977.

Reiss, D.: Pathways to assessing the family: Some choice points and a sample route. In Hofling, C.K., and Lewis, J.M. (Eds.): *The Family: Evaluation and Treatment.* New York: Brunner/Mazel Publishers. 1980.

Renshaw, D.C.: Impotence in diabetics. In LoPiccolo, J., and LoPiccolo, L. (Eds.): *Handbook of Sex Therapy.* New York: Plenum Press, 1978.

Rooney, D.D.: *Alcoholism and the Family.* CosCob, Connecticut: National Council on Alcoholism—Southwestern Connecticut Area, 1975.

Rubin, J., and Magnussen, M.G.: A family art evaluation. *Family Process, 13*: 185-200.

Rubinstein, D., and Weiner, O.R.: Co-therapy teamwork relationships in family therapy. In Zuk, G., and Boszormenyi-Nagy, I. (Eds.): *Family Therapy and Disturbed Families.* Palo Alto: Science and Behavior Books, 1967.

Sager, C.J., Masters, Y.J., Ronall, R.E., and Normand, W.C.: Selection and engagement of patients in family therapy. *American Journal of Orthopsychiatry, 38:*715-723, 1968.

Satir, V.: *Peoplemaking.* Palo Alto: Science and Behavior Books, 1972.

Satir, V.: *Conjoint Family Therapy.* Palo Alto: Science and Behavior Books, 1964.

Schuckit, M.S.: The alcoholic woman: A literature review. *Psychiatry in Medicine, 3:*37-43, 1972.

Shapiro, R.J.: A family therapy approach to alcoholism. *Journal of Marriage and Family Counseling, (October):*71-79, 1977.

Simon, R.: Sculpting the family. *Family Process, 11:*49-59, 1972.

Smith, R.S., and Alexander, A.M.: *Counseling Couples in Groups.* Springfield, Illinois: Thomas, 1974.

Solomon, M.A.: A developmental conceptual premise for family therapy. *Family Process, 12:*179-188, 1973.

Stanton, M.D., and Todd, T.C.: *Engaging "Resistant" Families in Treatment: II. Some Principles Gained in Recruiting Addict Families.* Unpublished monograph mailed to author): Philadelphia: Philadelphia Child Guidance Clinic, 1980.

Steinglass, P.: Experimenting with family treatment approaches to alcoholism, 1950-1975: A review. *Family Process, 15*(1):97-123, 1976.

Stierlin, H.: *Separating Parents and Adolescents.* New York: Quadrangle Press, 1974.

Stierlin, H.: *Psychoanalysis and Family Therapy.* New York: Jason Aronson, 1977.

Strack, J.H., and Dutton, L.A.: A new approach in the treatment of the married alcoholic. *Selected Papers, Twenty-Second Annual Meeting; Alcohol and Drug Problems Association of North America.* Hartford, Connecticut: (September 12-17, 1971).

Straus, R., and Bacon, S.D.: Alcoholism and social stability: A study of occupational integration in 2,023 male alcoholics. *Quarterly Journal of Studies on Alcohol, 12:*231-260, 1951.

Stuart, R.B.: Behavioral contracting within the families of delinquents. *Journal of Behavior Therapy and Experimental Psychiatry, 2:*1-11, 1971.

Towle, L.H.: Alcoholism treatment outcome in different populations. *Proceedings from the Fourth Annual Alcohol Conference of the NIAAA.* April, 1974.

VanDensen, J.M. et al.: *Engaging "Resistant" Families in Treatment: I. Getting the Drug Addict to Recruit His Family Members.* Paper submitted for publication, 1979.

Volpe, J.: Links to sobriety. *Alcohol Health and Research World, 4:*39-44, 1978-1980.

Watzlawick, P.: A structural family interview. *Family Process, 5:*256-271, 1966.

Watzlawick, P., Weakland, J.H., and Fish, R.: *Change: Principles of Problem Formation and Problem Solution.* New York: Norton, 1974.

Weakland, J. et al.: Brief therapy: Focused problem resolution. *Family Process,* 1974, pp. 114-168.

Whalen, T.: Wives of alcoholics: Four types observed in a family service agency. *Quarterly Journal of Studies on Alcohol, 14*:632-641, 1953.

Whitaker, C.: The growing edge. In Haley, J., and Hoffman, L. (Eds.): *Techniques of Family Therapy.* New York: Basic Books, 1967.

Whitaker, C.: The symptomatic adolescent—An awol family member. In Sugar, M.: *The Adolescent in Group and Family Therapy.* New York: Brunner/Mazel, 1975.

Yalom, I: *The Theory and Practice of Group Psychiatry.* New York: Basic Books, 1970.

Zuk, G.H.: *Family Therapy: A Triadic Based Approach.* New York: Quadrangle Press, 1974.

Zuk, G.H.: *Process and Practice in Family Therapy.* Haverford, Pennsylvania: Psychiatry and Behavioral Science Books, 1975.

INDEX